LOVERS AT VERSAILLES

THE SPIRIT OF ANNIE ROSS

The Arts Council
An Chomhairle Ealaíon

The publishers gratefully acknowledge the financial assistance
of the Arts Council/An Chomhairle Ealaíon

First published in 2002 by Marino Books
16 Hume Street Dublin 2
Tel: (01) 661 5299; Fax: (01) 661 8583
E-mail: books@marino.ie
An imprint of Mercier Press
5 French Church Street Cork
Tel: (021) 275040; Fax: (021) 274969
E-mail: books@mercier.ie
Website: www.mercier.ie
Trade enquiries to CMD Distribution
55A Spruce Avenue
Stillorgan Industrial Park
Blackrock County Dublin
Tel: (01) 294 2556; Fax: (01) 294 2564
E.mail: cmd@columba.ie

© Bernard Farrell 2002

ISBN 1 85635 390 7
10 9 8 7 6 5 4 3 2 1

A CIP record for this title is available
from the British Library
Cover design by Mercier Press
Cover illustration of Tina Kellegher
courtesy of Paul McCarthy
Printed in Ireland by ColourBooks,
Baldoyle Industrial Estate, Dublin 13

LOVERS AT VERSAILLES

THE SPIRIT OF ANNIE ROSS

BERNARD FARRELL

MERCIER PRESS

Contents

LOVERS AT VERSAILLES

This play was first presented at the Abbey Theatre, Dublin, on 6 March 2002, with the following cast:

ANNA	Tina Kellegher
ISOBEL	Rénee Weldon
DAVID	Barry Barnes/Sean Rocks
TONY	Keith McErlean
CLARA	Barbara Brennan
STEPHEN	Vincent McCabe
SANDRA	Victoria King
STEPHANIE	Jeananne Crowley
RITA	Gail Fitzpatrick
CLUBBERS/GYM MEMBERS	Gail Fitzpatrick
	Louise Kiely
	Victoria King
	Mick Mulcahy
	Douglas Rankine
DIRECTOR	Mark Lambert
DESIGNER	Joe Vanek
LIGHTING	Rupert Murray

for Gloria

ACT ONE

In a tight pool of light, Anna and Isobel sit at a table. A wine bottle and two empty glasses are on the table. This area is a detail of the larger Serendipity Club. It is noisy and crowded; however, we are only aware of the crowd by the shadowy people who move, drink or dance beyond the perimeter of this lighted area.

Anna is forty and her sister Isobel is thirty-five, but in this memory sequence of ten years ago, both behave younger than they look. Isobel is more attractive, assured and volatile; Anna is quieter and less adventurous. Both wear somewhat sombre clothes. Anna is ill at ease (even angry). Isobel is merrily in her element determined to enjoy herself.

Anna	*(Annoyed)* Never again.
Isobel	*(Impatient)* What?
Anna	This! This place! Not if you paid me a million pounds.
Isobel	What's up with you?
Anna	Noise, smoke, surrounded by drips peering at you from the gloom. It's a nightmare.
Isobel	For God's sake, relax. This is why it's called the Serendipity Club. You know what serendipity

means, don't you? *(Waves to someone in the dark)*
Hi, Tommy . . . love the tie.

In response, 'Tommy' makes his tie light up in the darkness – to the delight of Isobel.

Anna	Should be called the Seren*drip*ity Club.
Isobel	*(Merrily)* Serendipity means that surprising things can happen to you – and they will, if you let them.
1st male	*(Voice from the dark)* Hi, sexy.
Isobel	Oh hi, Peter.
1st male	Tony not with you?
Isobel	At the bar, getting us drinks.
1st male	OK, see ya later. *(Going)*
Isobel	By the way, this is my sister Anna . . .
Anna	*(Furious)* For God's sake!
First male	*(Looks at Anna)* It's OK, no problem, see ya. *(Gone)*
Anna	What are you now – a pimp?
Isobel	Well, if you're not going to make a move yourself . . .
Anna	I will make a move – back to the house.
Isobel	*(Annoyed)* Oh, you'd prefer to be at home with mammy and daddy, watching *The Late Late Show?* The three of you sitting there like the Three Bears.
Anna	Oh thanks!
2nd male	*(From the shadows)* Enjoying it, Isobel?
Isobel	Fabulous. Did you see Tony anywhere?
2nd male	Is he here?

Isobel	Went to the bar. If you see him, tell him we're nursing an empty bottle here.
2nd male	Will do. *(Goes)*
Isobel	By the way, this is my . . .
Anna	*(Angrily)* Don't!
Isobel	He's gone anyway. And who'd blame him – that face of yours would scatter a herd of elephants.
Anna	Thank you!
Isobel	I'm only saying it for your own good. You're nearly thirty, Anna.
Anna	Why don't you put it on a placard over my head?
Isobel	I'm just saying, I'm five years younger and already I have Tony with his tongue out on his chest like a little . . . *(Suddenly)* Oh God, don't look, but there's that peculiar fella again, eyeing me up.
Anna	*(Peering)* Where?
Isobel	I said don't look!
Anna	I can't see anyone.
Isobel	Stripping me naked – bloody pervert!
Anna	Will I get Tony?
Isobel	And leave me on my own! God, he's coming over.
Anna	Maybe we should just go?
Isobel	*(Anxiously)* Too late. Don't leave me. No matter what happens, you stay there. Do you hear me? Do you, do you?!
Anna	Yes! Yes! Yes! God.

David comes into the pool of light. He is, in this memory, aged thirty. He is a big man, but gentle and ill at ease.

David	*(To Anna)* Hello.

Isobel	*(Coldly)* I'm sorry – my boyfriend is with me – getting us drinks – back any moment now.
David	Oh, right. *(To Anna)* Hello, I hope you don't mind, but I've been looking at you, wondering if we met before. My name is David. *(Extends his hand)*
Anna	*(Taken off guard)* What? Oh, how do you do? *(Shakes hands briefly)* I'm Annabelle.
David	Annabelle? That's a lovely name.
Anna	Thank you. And this is my sister, Isobel.
David	*(Amused)* Isobel ?
Isobel	*(Coldly)* Hi.
David	Annabelle and Isobel?
Anna	*(Lightly)* Yes, and our mother's full name is Clarabelle.
Isobel	*(Angrily)* For God's sake!
David	*(Relaxing)* And don't tell me – your father's name is Jingle Bell?
Anna	*(Amused)* No, actually he's Stephen.
David	So you two and your mother are the only belles in the house?
Anna	*(Merrily)* Yes – except for the one on the front door.
David	Oh, very good.
Isobel	God!
David	*(To Anna)* And I really do know you from somewhere. Don't worry, it'll come to me.

An awkward silence. But David stays.

Anna	And do you like this place?
Isobel	*(Through her teeth)* Will you let him go!

14

David	Here? Oh yes, it's good, great – and really great furniture. They've spent money in here. Have you noticed the tables?
Anna	The tables? No.
David	That's pure teak and, if you look carefully, all those joints are perfectly dovetailed, not a screw to be seen anywhere.
Anna	*(Looking at the table)* Really?
David	And have you noticed the dance floor?
Isobel	*(Coldly)* I'd say there's a few screws out there.
David	*(Seriously)* That's the point, Clarabelle.
Isobel	Isobel!
David	... Isobel, every inch of that floor is pure maple-wood, all in interlocking, five-inch, dove-tailed panels, and the full unit internally supported and balanced. That's great craftsmanship, that floor.
Anna	You're not a carpenter, are you?
Isobel	*(Quietly)* Or a lunatic.
David	Right first time, Annabelle – following in my father's footsteps.
Anna	He makes tables and floors, does he?
David	No no. Don't laugh – he actually specialises in making coffins.
Isobel	Jesus Christ!
Anna	*(Seriously)* Does he really? Coffins?
David	Oh yes. I help him out, but eventually I want to move into more general carpentry. I love the business. Since I was that high, I was always carving things out of wood. At present I'm carving a snow goose, as an ornament.

15

Anna	Oh, lovely.
David	Just in my spare time – get me away from the coffins for a while. And now I have you!
Anna	Pardon?
David	You work in that grocery shop – Sullivan's. That's where I've seen you.
Anna	Oh yes, that's our father's shop.
David	Oh, is he the oul' fel . . . the man that's always with you?
Anna	Yes, that's daddy.
David	And do you work there too, Isobel?
Isobel	*(Coldly)* No, I don't.
Anna	Isobel is a dental receptionist.
Isobel	Dental assistant!
David	Oh, right. Teeth. Great.

Another awkward silence. But David stays. The music now is Sinatra singing 'Strangers in the Night'.

Anna	I love that – 'Strangers in the Night'.
David	*(Enthusiastic)* Are you serious? That's my favourite song of all time.
Anna	*(Enthusiastic)* Really? Honestly?
David	Yes! It's actually my party piece. Any time I'm asked to sing, that's what I sing.
Anna	*(Listening)* It's brilliant.
David	I do the 'Do-be-do-be-do' bit and everything.
Isobel	Christ! *(Then, calls)* Tony? Tony? Over here, Toe.

Tony comes into the light. He holds a drink. He is well-dressed, fit and confident and, in this memory, aged twenty-three.

Tony	*(To Isobel)* You OK, sweetheart?
Isobel	Darling, where's our drinks?
Tony	*(Kissing Isobel)* OK, getting them now, sexy – don't panic.
Isobel	*(Coolly)* But it's been ten minutes since . . .
Tony	*(More passionate)* I got, ya know, distracted.
Isobel	*(Embarrassed)* Tony! We have company!
Tony	*(Still kissing)* Anna doesn't mind.
Isobel	And! *(Indicates David standing nearby)*
Tony	*(Stops)* Oh, hello. Thought you were, ya know, just standing there.
David	No, I'm talking too.
Anna	Tony, this is David.
Tony	How ya. And you're, ya know, with Anna, are you?
David and Anna	
	(Together) No, no!
Isobel	No, no! He just came over . . . and stayed. He makes coffins.
Tony	Pardon?
David	No, my father does. I just help.
Tony	Coffins? For dead people?
Anna	*(Colder)* Yes, Tony, he's a carpenter. It's what carpenters do!
Tony	Oh right. *(Little joke)* Long as you're not here looking for business.
David	*(Seriously)* No, no, I came over because I recognised Annabelle from the shop.
Tony	Who? Oh, Anna. Right.
David	Are you connected with the shop, Tony?
Tony	Me?
Isobel	You don't know who Tony is?

17

Tony	*(Proudly)* Ever go to see the Hoops playing?
Anna	Tony plays football, David – for Shamrock Rovers.
David	Oh, sorry. I don't actually . . .
Tony	*(Annoyed)* It's OK – no sweat.
Isobel	God, he really doesn't know who Tony is!
David	I'm sorry, I've no interest in . . .
Isobel	You didn't read in the papers that Tony is going for a trial at Leeds?
David	A trial? Why, what's he done?
Tony	Jaysus, I'll get the drinks.
David	Oh, in football? Sorry.
Tony	You staying here, David, or going?
David	Oh, if it's OK, I'll stay – but I'll get these . . .
Tony	No, no, you're all right . . . *(Going)*
David	No, I'd like to . . .
Tony	Just tell me what you want.
David	I'll help you back with them then . . .
Tony	Right. *(To Anna and Isobel, as he goes)* If I'm not back in five minutes, check for my body in the morgue!

Tony and David leave the pool of light.

Isobel	What's got into you with that weirdo?
Anna	He's not a weirdo.
Isobel	Oh, it's normal to be examining the dance floor for screws, is it?
Anna	Well, what is 'normal' in this place?
Isobel	We'll never get rid of him now.

Anna picks up the bottle and pours a glass of red wine.

Isobel	*(Looking at Anna pouring)* Are you not thinking of going to bed soon?
Anna	What?
Isobel	You said ten minutes ago you felt like going to bed.
Anna	With David? I never said that.
Isobel	*(Aghast)* David? Who's David?

The lights suddenly change, all music and sounds stop. The spot of light broadens out . . . and we are in the present day, in the sitting room of Anna's house. Anna and Isobel at the table, with the glasses and the bottle of wine. The door from the hall is at stage left, the door to the kitchen at stage right. The door in the back wall leads to the shop beyond. All doors are closed. The sitting room has a slightly old-fashioned feel to it – showing the influence of older people living here: Anna's mother and father. Usual furniture, including a television. It is late evening. When Isobel stands, we see that she is pregnant.

Anna	*(Back from her memory. Confused)* Pardon? Sorry, Isobel, what did you say?
Isobel	*(Amused)* You said 'David'.
Anna	No, I didn't. *You* said . . .
Isobel	You *did* say David.
Anna	*(Anxiously)* No, you asked was I going to bed with him, and I . . .
Isobel	*(More serious)* With who? Why would I ask such a thing?
Anna	But you did!
Isobel	Anna, you're getting worse.
Anna	*(Confused)* No, I was thinking and . . .

19

Isobel	*(Annoyed)* You sit there in total silence for half an hour – I assume you're thinking about daddy dying or how mammy is going to cope, and then you suddenly come out with wanting to go to bed with some David!
Anna	No, I didn't – *you* said that!
Isobel	Is this David O'Gorman, by any chance?
Anna	What? No. Well, yes, but I didn't say . . .
Isobel	Oh, Anna!
Anna	No, no, it was just that something reminded me of the Serendipity Club, and . . .
Isobel	The Serendipity Club? That's gone nearly ten years – and so is David O'Gorman.
Anna	I know that, I was just . . .
Isobel	*(Mock amusement)* Sometimes, Anna, I wish I could see into that head of yours.
Anna	*(Harder)* Well, you haven't been *here* to see into this head of mine, or anyone else's head.
Isobel	I know, but we're here now – and don't you worry, Tony and I will be staying for as long as it takes.
Anna	As long as *what* takes?
Isobel	All this – daddy's funeral, what mammy will do, what happens to this house, what happens to the shop, what happens to you . . .
Anna	Me? I'm fine – and I'll be opening the shop again on Thursday . . .
Isobel	Oh don't be silly, Anna – Tony and I are happy to stay until . . .
Anna	But you have your life in Leeds . . .
Isobel	Leeds can wait – Jason and Kate can be taken out of school, Tony's health club practically runs

itself and, if needs be, I can get a dental position here. *(Taps her pregnancy)* And maybe this little chap will be born in Ireland. *(Sadly)* Poor daddy. *(Then angrily)* That bloody shop – and he knew where that trapdoor was. *(Sadly)* And poor you finding him at the bottom, trying to revive him.

Anna   He was dead then – there was nothing I could do.

Isobel   I know. And poor mammy having to come back to that.

Anna   *(Harder)* She should never have gone in the first place.

Isobel   Now, Anna, don't take sides – she's not well. Tony and I have seen great changes in her since we were last over. *(Listens. A sound)* She's moving around. I think she's gone in to see him again.

Anna   He shouldn't be here at all – there's a perfectly good funeral home . . .

Isobel   Oh, I hate those places and so does mammy. They're like Madame Tussaud's: a body here, a body there – oh look, there's another body over there. This is more dignified: in his own home, among his own. *(Listens)* I think she's coming down.

Anna   *(Coldy)* For more cigarettes and a drop of tay – her cure for everything.

Isobel   Yes, poor thing.

The stage-left door opens. Clara – Clarabelle - comes in. She is in her sixties, looking tired and weary.

Clara   This is where you are.

21

Isobel	Yes, mammy, remembering the good old days.
Clara	All well and truly gone now. Never a cigarette anywhere when you want one.
Anna	*(Stands)* I can get you some from the shop.
Clara	I can get them! *(Gets the key and goes to the shop door)* I was in this shop long before any of you ever were.
Isobel	I think I saw a packet in that drawer, mammy.
Clara	*(Replaces the key. Gets cigarettes from drawer. Towards Anna)* Still nearly have to ask permission to go into that cursed shop.

Clara lights a cigarette. Anna sits again.

Isobel	And mammy, do you think there'll be any more calling this evening to see . . . for the wake?
Clara	You mean will that woman dare to show her face?
Isobel	No, no, mammy, not her. I mean anyone – neighbours.
Clara	Who knows? I'll be staying up a while longer anyway – no chance of sleeping tonight. Is Tony gone to bed?
Isobel	No, mammy, he went to the pub, just to see his old friends.
Clara	From the football?
Isobel	Yes, it's been a long time. But he's very sad about daddy, said he needed to get away for just an hour or so. He really loved daddy.
Clara	I know he did – and your father was very fond of him too.
Isobel	Yes. And how do you think he's looking, mammy?

22

Clara	To tell the truth, I wouldn't have recognised him.
Isobel	Really?
Clara	There's something the matter with his mouth, it's all twisted to one side and his hair is brushed completely different, whoever brushed it that way.
Isobel	Well actually, he brushed it that way himself.
Clara	How could he brush it himself? He's dead.
Isobel	What? Oh you're talking about daddy, are you, mammy?
Clara	Why, who else is dead. Is there another body somewhere else in the house, another shock waiting for me, is there – to finish me all completely?
Isobel	No, no, mammy – I was talking about Tony!
Clara	Tony is grand, a lovely-looking fellow – the best son-in-law I could have, giving me my two lovely grandchildren.
Isobel	And soon this one, mammy. *(Referring to her pregnancy)*
Clara	Oh, if I live to see it, after the heartbreak of all this. Get a drop of tay for myself.

Clara goes into the kitchen at stage right.

Isobel	She'll miss daddy so much.
Anna	Miss spying on him.
Isobel	Now Anna!
Anna	*(Annoyed)* And you can't pretend she didn't do that – always insisting he kept that door open.

23

(The shop door)

Isobel	*(Annoyed)* Only because of how he used to go on, chatting up his lady-friends, knowing she was listening . . .
Anna	They were our customers!
Isobel	. . . and annoying her, boasting how lovely they all were.
Anna	He was joking!
Isobel	*(Angrily)* Some jokes! And Anna, I know he's dead and we are all devastated, but he could be the most annoying man.
Anna	He never annoyed me.
Isobel	Oh really? So you've forgotten things like the day David O'Gorman first came to the house?
Anna	For God's sake!
Isobel	Yes, Anna, remember the pig's teeth and calling him Daniel and all the questions about coffins.
Anna	They were jokes!
Isobel	You didn't think so at the time.
Anna	Yes I did.
Isobel	See? That's your whole trouble, Anna – you forget everything. Is it any wonder that we all worry what's going to happen to you now?

A sound from the kitchen.

Isobel	I'll see if mammy's all right.

Isobel goes into the kitchen, taking the wine bottle and glasses. She closes the kitchen door. A moment. Anna sits remembering . . . and now the sound of a tinkling piano and a change

*of lights, establishing this first flashback. Anna sits facing us,
smiling at this memory as the area beyond the back wall is
illuminated and we see, in her memory, the shop, as though the
wall were not there. (A gauze to be used for the back wall,
allowing us to reveal or conceal the shop by use of lights. Never
a backdrop or scenery flat.)*

*It is a well-stocked shop, selling everything from sliced ham
to bundles of firewood. Stephen, in his sixties and wearing a
brown overall, tends to the last customer, then good-humouredly
sees her out through the upstage door, onto the street. He locks and
bolts the door, checks the trapdoor on the floor. He is removing his
overall as he speaks.*

*When he comes into the sitting room, the shop will fade,
but will still be seen, dimly.*

Stephen	Right, Annabelle, all set to meet your Daniel.
Anna	*(Lightly)* Daddy, his name is David, and he's not mine.
Stephen	He soon will be, if we play our cards right. You just leave all the talking to me.
Anna	No, daddy, mammy doesn't want that. Isobel and mammy say they will do the talking and, no matter what happens, nobody is to ask what David does for a living.
Stephen	He makes coffins, doesn't he?
Anna	Daddy, we're not saying that.
Stephen	And why not? He's not out murdering people to put into them, is he? *(Puts on a smart jacket)*
Anna	No, he's not, but mammy doesn't like it and neither does Isobel. Instead, Isobel will casually bring up about Tony's football career and we'll

25

talk about that.

Stephen gets a tin containing shoe-polishing materials from the corner of the room. Will now diligently polish his shoes, as:

Stephen	Oh, the new Georgie Best, God help us – well, I'm going to say that I've seen that yahoo playing and I can tell you he couldn't kick snow off a rope.
Anna	You're not to say that, daddy – and not to mention the word coffin either.
Stephen	And supposing Daniel mentions it?
Anna	That's all right, it seems – if he mentions it, then we can talk about it. And his name is not Daniel, it's David – think of David and Goliath.
Stephen	Oh, right. And only if he mentions the coffins – and I sincerely hope he does, because I want to ask him, in his experience, about the chances of someone being buried alive . . . *(With feeling)* . . . of being in a coffin, in the dark, suddenly waking up and realising they're not dead and then scratching like mad on the inside of the lid and nobody noticing . . .
Anna	Daddy!
Stephen	It's a fear everyone has, Anna, and he might have encountered it, might have heard the scratching at the last minute, had to open up the coffin . . . *(Sees Anna's look)* . . . But I know, I know – it's all only if he mentions the word first. How am I looking – all right?

26

Anna	You look great. And not too many of your jokes, daddy.
Stephen	Don't worry – me best behaviour. *(Puts the shoe-polish tin away)*
Anna	And I think you'll like him.
Stephen	Of course I will. Why wouldn't I? Oh, nearly forgot – get a few bottles of beer I left in the fridge. *(Going towards the kitchen)*
Anna	No, daddy, mammy says no alcohol. We're having tea.
Stephen	*(Stops)* Tea? Jaysus, Anna, I can't operate drinking tea – me throat will get all dried up. I'll need a glass in my hand. I'm afraid, Anna, I'm going to have to insist on drinking me beer.

The kitchen door opens. Clara comes in with a tray of cups, saucers and tea. She is ten years younger in this flashback, well-dressed and confident.

Clara	Now, tea for everyone.
Stephen	Fair enough, Clara.
Anna	Mammy, he's not here yet – it'll be cold.
Clara	If he's interested, he'll be on time. I'll get some Kimberley and Marie biscuits from the shop.
Stephen	I'll get them, Clara.
Clara	*(Angrily)* For God's sake – I'll put the money in, you'll still balance.
Stephen	It's not that, Clara. *(Going)*
Clara	You think you're the only one that can work that till.
Stephen	Not at all – it's just that we've moved the

	biscuits. One Marie, one Kimberley. *(Goes into the shop)*
Clara	*(Calls angrily)* And how did I study nursing for three years if I'm supposed to be so stupid?

Clara puts out the cups.

Anna	And mammy, can we all just be normal? David is only dropping in for five minutes.
Clara	If you wanted it to be 'normal', why is your father here?
Anna	Daddy will be all right. I've spoken to him, and he won't mention David's occupation unless David says it first.
Clara	Well, we'll see. But don't you go blaming me if this fella disappears like the rest.
Anna	The rest? What rest?
Clara	Oh, good question! You out in that shop day in and day out, meeting fella after fella – and nothing. It took Isobel to get you out to meet this one.
Anna	Isobel had nothing to do with this.
Clara	And look at you now, not even dressed up.
Anna	Because it's supposed to be casual, normal, relaxed, for God's sake.
Clara	You should take a leaf from Isobel's book.
Anna	Oh God, what's she wearing?
Clara	Never mind what she's wearing. Isobel is used to dealing with professional people in the dental profession. She knows how to put people at their ease, how to converse and open up

28

intelligent conversations – not the nonsensical talk you hear across that counter out there.

Stephen comes in with two packets of biscuits.

Stephen	Here we are: one Kimberly, one Marie.
Clara	I'll put those out here.
Stephen	And Clara, I might get a few bottles of beer I left in . . . *(Towards the kitchen)*
Clara	What did you say?
Stephen	*(Stops)* It's just that my chest is very wheezy.
Clara	Well, you can un-wheeze it with a nice cup of tea.
Stephen	*(Quietly)* But tea only makes it worse.

The doorbell rings.

Anna	That'll be him. *(Going)*
Clara	Anna, stay where you are!
Anna	But that's him at the door.
Clara	Isobel is answering the door.
Anna	What?
Clara	It's all arranged – Isobel will know what to say, how to greet him.
Anna	Oh, for God's sake!
Clara	And you should be grateful she's here to help you out.
Anna	And why's she not answering the door now?
Clara	Will you calm down! She will when he rings a second time.
Anna	What?

The doorbell rings again.

Clara   There. We'll do this properly.

Anna   Good God, it's like a military operation.

Stephen   And we won't shoot till we see the whites of his eyes.

Clara   And Stephen Sullivan, let that be the last of those ignorant comments.

Voices – and the sound of Isobel laughing – are heard outside the door.

Clara   Here they are. Now, Anna, you stand there and *(To Stephen)* let us all be sensible and relaxed and supporting Anna at all times – and please God something will come of this.

Stage-left door opens. Isobel, in a sexy dress, enters with David. He is carrying a bag containing a carving of a snow goose in flight, as a gift. Isobel is laughing too much at something that David said. Her accent is now more upmarket. Clara sits waiting. Stephen looking almost too relaxed – until silently corrected by Clara.

Isobel   *(Laughing)* Oh, that is so funny, David – you know, you really are so witty.

David   *(Laughing)* But it's true. *(To Anna)* Hello.

Anna   Hello, David. Mammy, this is David O'Gorman.

Clara   Ah, David, how lovely to meet you, and how nice of you to drop by. We were about to have tea . . . you'll join us, I hope?

David   Oh, thank you very much.

Clara   Yes, we always have tea about this time.

David	Great. And a little something for the house. *(Takes the snow goose from the bag)*
Anna	Oh, lovely. Mammy, David carved this himself.
David	Just in my spare time.
Clara	*(Lost but trying hard)* Well, it's magnificent, wonderful. Thank you. Look, Stephen.
Stephen	Oh, lovely. It's a duck, is it?
David	Well, a snow goose actually.
Clara	*(U-turn)* Of course it's a snow goose!
Isobel	Of course!
Stephen	Oh, I see it now. That'd go lovely in the shop, Anna – above the fridge.
Anna	Yes, daddy, it would. Oh, sorry, daddy – this is David. David, my father.
Stephen	Very pleased to meet you, David. I've been warned not to call you by that other name – Goliath.
David	Pardon me?
Stephen	No, no, sorry, it was Daniel I was thinking of.
David	Daniel? *(Lightly, to Anna)* And who is this Daniel?
Clara	*(Anxiously)* No, no, there is no Daniel…
Isobel	*(Anxiously)* No, no, there's no one else. Just you, David.
Clara	Daddy made a mistake, David – Daniel never existed.
Stephen	Oh, he existed all right.
Clara	*(Hard)* No, Stephen, he didn't.
Isobel	He didn't, daddy!
Stephen	He did, in the Bible. Wasn't he in the lions' den when . . .

Clara	No he wasn't, and David doesn't want to hear about anyone in a lions' den, so that's the end of that. Now, David, do you take milk and sugar?
David	Both, I'm afraid.
Clara	Oh my, isn't that a coincidence, Anna also takes milk and sugar – something else in common.
Anna	*(Annoyed)* I'm actually off sugar.
Clara	*(Quietly)* Then get back on it.
Stephen	And do you take a drink at all, Daniel?
Clara	There's your tea now, *David*. Now tell me, which do you prefer – Marie or Kimberley?
David	Marie? Who's Marie?
Clara	*(Getting the biscuits)* No, no – Marie the biscuit.
David	Oh, sorry. Marie would be lovely, thank you.
Clara	Very welcome. And a Kimberley too, and why not. *(Gives him one)*
David	Thank you.

An awkward pause as everyone tastes the tea. Stephen sips it and coughs.

Clara	All right, Stephen?
Stephen	Grand. Bit of a wheeze.
Clara	Lovely. And is Tony coming over, Isobel?
Isobel	No, actually he's training.
Clara	Of course. *(To David)* You know that Tony, one of Isobel's boyfriends, plays professional football for the First Division club, Shamrock Rovers?
David	Oh yes, so I've heard.
Clara	By all accounts he is excellent and has wonderful prospects.

Stephen	Although they were beaten four-nil by Bohemians on Sunday.
Clara	*(Coldly)* Really? Thank you for that, Stephen.
Isobel	*(Coldly)* Yes, daddy, thank you.

Pause

David	*(Awkwardly)* And the shop out there.
Clara	Oh yes – where you first met Anna, I believe?
David	Yes – and then at the Serendipity Club. They played 'Strangers in the Night' – which we both love.
Clara	Do I know that?
David	Oh yes, you know *(Sings)* 'Ever since that night we've been together, lovers at Versailles, in love forever.' *(Continues)* 'It turned out so right . . . ' *(Embarrassed)* . . . But I can't sing very well.
Stephen	*(Applauds)* No, you do – a lovely voice.
Clara	*(Applauds)* Oh yes, you do – as does Anna. I have often heard her out in the shop, when it's quiet. A lovely voice. *(Sees her amused look)* You have, Anna. And when I was doing my training – I trained as a nurse but never practised because I got married to him – I was always singing, always . . . mainly classical songs.
David	*(Pause. Awkwardly)* Great.
Clara	Isobel has to be a lot more serious in her profession, I'm afraid – Isobel is a dental assistant.
David	Oh yes, I heard.

An awkward silence. Clara looks to Isobel.

Clara	*(Cues her)* Isobel.
Isobel	*(Takes her cue)* Yes. And what I find most interesting in the profession of dentistry is their basic training – it is almost seven years, you know – and it is an amazing but little-known fact that dentists actually practise tooth-extraction by pulling out pigs' teeth, and the really captivating reason for this is that, in terms of genetic comparison, pigs' teeth are closest to the teeth of our own human teeth, the teeth of *Homo sapiens,* as we say, or, in plain English, mankind.
Stephen	Jaysus!
Clara	*(To cover up)* Now, David, isn't that most interesting?
David	Indeed. Absolutely.
Stephen	I never heard that before.
Clara	We learn something every day, Stephen.
Stephen	And would the pig be dead when they'd bring him in to have his teeth out?
Isobel	Of course, daddy. They'd come from the abattoir.
Clara	Brought in for medical research.
Stephen	Oh, right. And wouldn't a goat's teeth be just as good?
Isobel	No, daddy, it has to be a pig.
Stephen	Or a sheep's teeth, or a cow's, or a rabbit's . . . ?
Clara	*(Lightly)* Stephen, are we going to go through the entire litany of animals? You heard what Isobel said: pigs' teeth are the best.
David	I cannot tell you how much I dislike the dentist.
Clara	All people do – but it is essential that we go.

Isobel	And these days it is both pain-free and relaxing.
David	Excellent.
Stephen	*(Beat)* And when they're practising on the pig's teeth, would they have the pig's head all tied up to the dentist's chair with the light on it and all?
Clara	Of course not, Stephen. They wouldn't have it in the chair at all – they'd have the head like it is in the butchers.
Isobel	Although, mammy, it is terribly wrong to be comparing dentists to butchers.
Clara	Oh, of course, dear.
Isobel	Dentists are my closest friends and all of them are highly professional people.
Clara	Well of course they are – like the doctors I knew when I was doing my medical training. I was best friends with so many and all were highly professional.
Isobel	Exactly.
Stephen	Exactly. And now that I come to think of it, Isobel, you're absolutely right – human's heads can be exactly like pigs' heads. I've noticed that down in the pub of an evening – you see a fellow at closing time trying to finish his pint, and it all running down his mouth and him snorting into the glass to get it down as quick as he can so he can order another one – and you'd swear you were looking at a pig. So you're absolutely right there, Isobel.
Isobel	*(Coldly)* Thank you, daddy.

Pause

Clara	Another biscuit, David?
David	Oh, many thanks.

Stephen drinks his tea and coughs.

Clara	Are you all right, Stephen?
Stephen	Yes. Grand. *(To David)* Did you ever get an attack of that, David?
David	Do you mean coughing?
Stephen	*(Delighted)* Coffin, did you say? Oh right, we're away, he's said it. And you're in that business, aren't you – making coffins?
Clara	Stephen, David said 'coughing'.
Stephen	I know, I heard him. *(To David)* And as funerals and burials is your trade, so to speak . . .
Isobel	Daddy!
Stephen	. . . maybe you could confirm that it is a great fear of everyone to be put into a coffin while they are really still alive.
David	*(Amused)* Oh, absolutely.
Stephen	So you won't be too surprised to hear that I have left strict instructions that, when I die, before the lid goes on my coffin, I want someone to stick several sharp needles into my fingers and only if there is no reaction whatsoever from me, does the lid then go on, and no questions asked thereafter. A good precaution, Daniel?
David	An excellent one, I'd say.
Stephen	*(To all)* There you are – and that's from someone on the inside, so to speak.
Clara	Thank you, Stephen – and now maybe you'd

36

	show David the shop. *(To David)* For you to see it from the other side of the counter, David.
David	Oh that would be lovely, Mrs Sullivan.
Clara	Excellent. Then lead on, Stephen. *(To David)* And it is Clara, David.
David	Oh thank you, Clara.
Stephen	This way, David. *(Picks up the snow goose)* And we'll bring the duck.
Clara	*(Corrects)* The snow goose!
Stephen	Oh, right. See how it looks in here. *(Going into the shop, carrying the snow goose)* Let me just make sure the trapdoor is closed.

Lights up to normal in the shop, as Stephen leads David in. Clara, Isobel and Anna will quickly clear the table, Isobel taking all off to the kitchen on a tray, and then returning. All as:

Clara	Now, it's going very well so far. But, Anna, you have to speak, you have to say something.
Anna	Like what?
Clara	Like anything – or David will think you've been struck dumb.
Isobel	I think he's enjoying it – even singing!
Clara	As long as your father remembers to conduct himself. And Anna – don't forget to talk!

Clara goes to the shop. Isobel follows from the kitchen. Anna waits in the sitting room, watching, remembering what we hear and see.

Clara	*(Entering the shop)* Now, Stephen can demonstrate how he can remember where everything is.

Isobel	*(Enthusiastic)* Oh yes, David, this is such fun – we used to do this when we were children. You ask daddy something and see if he knows exactly where it is and how much it costs. You go first. Anything at all.
David	Right. So . . . where are the cigarettes?
Stephen	*(Indicating)* That's easy, there, two-pound-eighty cheapest . . . Matches twelve pee, there . . . Disposable lighters over there, one pound each.
Isobel	See?
David	Wonderful.
Clara	And the Bird's Jelly, Stephen?
Stephen	There, forty-five pee a packet, and custard there and eggs over there, and eggcups down here.
Isobel	And the toothpaste, daddy?
Stephen	Right there, from ninety-nine pee . . . indigestion tablets there . . . and Dettol there.
David	That's great.
Clara	There's nothing he can't find and price.
Stephen	And most important, David, in a crisis – the toilet rolls are over there, Andrex at two-twenty for a packet of four. Or there's a cheaper, rougher kind . . .
Clara	*(Quickly)* Never mind that, Stephen – where is the Persil?
Stephen	Persil? To the right, top shelf, two fifty-nine. You know, Anna is just as good at this.
David	Where is Anna? I'll get her in.
Isobel	*(To Stephen)* And daddy, where are the cashew nuts, the hazelnuts and the peanuts.

| Stephen | *(Laughs)* Right there beside the fruit-and-nuts. *(Indicates Clara and Isobel)* |

Lughter at this – as Stephen continues (now mimed) and David comes from the shop to Anna.

David	*(Excited)* Anna, this is great! *(Then)* I didn't say something wrong, did I?
Anna	*(Lovingly)* Indeed you didn't.
David	Your dad is great – come on and hear him.
Anna	*(Amused)* Darling, just one thing. Why do you always sing 'Lovers at Versailles, in love forever'?
David	Because it's my party piece.
Anna	But they're the wrong words. It's 'Lovers at first sight'.
David	First sight? No, Versailles – lovers at Versailles – romance.
Anna	No, David.
David	*(Amused)* It is. I ought to know, Anna.
Anna	I'll buy you the record.
David	OK, let's do that, and you'll find that I'm right.
Anna	Oh, and Frank Sinatra is wrong?
David	No, Frank and I are right, *you're* wrong! Come on – I love this shop. *(Goes back into the shop, excitedly)*
Anna	*(Calls)* So do I. *(More gently)* And you too.

The stage-left door has opened and Tony has come in. He stands watching Anna.

| Anna | *(Still remembering)* And I loved you too. |

Tony closes the door and, at this sound, Anna sees him — and immediately all lights change and the shop-lights go out and the back wall is again in place. We are back to the present day. Tony is dressed in a suit, the tie undone. Although he has been to the pub, he is not drunk. He is finishing a cigarette.

Anna	Tony.
Tony	Anna. Isobel in or out?
Anna	In the kitchen, making tea with mammy.
Tony	Oh right, I won't disturb then. But were you, ya know, talking to someone in here?
Anna	Me? No. Just thinking.
Tony	Right. Understand. And my sincere condolences again.
Anna	Tony, every time you see me you say that, and it's not necessary – I know I have your sincere condolences.
Tony	Oh, right. Nice to see my old pals again, down in my old local . . . the years go by . . . some doing well, some not . . . but a lot of envy there.
Anna	Really?
Tony	Oh yes. But I'm used to it. First my cross-channel football career and now my own health club over there – success breeds envy.
Anna	I expect so.

Pause

Tony	And any more visitors come to see the bod . . . to see your da?
Anna	No. Getting late now.

40

Tony	Right. And no sign of herself?
Anna	Who?
Tony	Ya know, his . . . lady-friend – Hilary, Heather – Harriet, wasn't that her name?
Anna	Nobody called since you left . . . except Mrs Regan from next door.
Tony	Oh, the cake shop? Right. Very upset, was she?
Anna	Yes. As we all are.
Tony	Of course, of course, understandable. And my sincere condolences again. *(Realises)* Sorry.

Pause. But no sign of Tony going.

Tony	And strangely, being here at this sad time gives me a chance to say, Anna, that I often think back to other days. Like we all thought that you and the coffin-maker would have made a go of it – maybe even beaten Isobel and me to the altar. David, wasn't it?
Anna	Yes.
Tony	I often think of him – David. And I think about you too – I mean as a sister-in-law – like what's going to become of you now? All right, I know, I hate that word 'spinster' as much as anyone, but we have to face up to it that life has its hazards for any woman in that situation, out in the world on her own, and, in that regard, I do have a word of advice for you.
Anna	Do you?
Tony	Well, two words.
Anna	I hope they're not 'sincere condolences'.

41

Tony	No no – they're 'self-defence'.
Anna	Self-defence?
Tony	I happen to give instruction in the art of self-defence in my health club – and no woman, married or single, but especially single, should be without it, in my opinion. For example, have you noticed a new confidence in Isobel?
Anna	Well . . .
Tony	That's because I have taught her everything she knows about self-defence. And now, if she's out with her mates, do I worry? Not in the least. The truth is that Isobel can deal with any man – she could even floor me in two fast moves, no trouble to her. And that'd be my recommendation to you, Anna, because of your, ya know, circumstances, because of what is likely to become of you now.
Anna	Well, thank you.
Tony	No problem. And I'd also like to give you some advice about that shop out there.

The stage-right kitchen door opens. Isobel and Clara come out.

Clara	*(Angrily, to Isobel)* The question has to be asked, Isobel, even if it kills me.
Isobel	I know, mammy, but . . . *(Sees Tony)* Oh, Tony!
Tony	Hello, love, just back – giving some recommendations to Anna about . . .
Isobel	*(Hard)* Very good, but I think that first, Tony, we should deal with daddy's funeral and mammy's wishes, before any recommendations.

42

Tony	Oh, absolutely. And once again, Clara, my sincere condolences.
Clara	Thank you, again, Tony.
Tony	No problem . . . and you should be resting, you know – tomorrow is a big day for you . . . well, not a big day – it's a funeral . . . but, ya know.
Clara	I know, Tony – though God knows how I'll get through it.
Isobel	You'll be grand, mammy, and we'll make sure all your wishes are carried out. And Tony, mammy says she would like you to carry daddy's coffin.
Tony	When, now?
Isobel	*(Angrily)* Now? Where are you going to carry it now? Daddy's not even in it.
Tony	Oh tomorrow, at the church? Right, no problem. And there'll be others carrying it too, I presume?
Clara	*(Weary)* Tony, I'm not asking you to carry it on your back.
Tony	No, course not – many hands make . . . *(Stops)*
Clara	Thank you, Tony.
Tony	No problem, Clara, I'll take care of that – and meantime, you know you have my sincere . . .
Anna	Condolences.
Tony	Exactly.
Clara	Thank you again, Tony – and the way I feel this minute, you could be carrying my own coffin very soon after that.
Tony	No problem – a pleasure any time.
Isobel	Tony!
Tony	*(Quickly)* Except that won't be for a long time yet.
Clara	Don't be so sure, with what I'm slowly learning

about the private life of that man up there. So, Isobel, after the removal to the church tomorrow, we will have house-private and then, at the funeral mass on Wednesday, I'd like you to do all the readings.

Isobel   Not Sister Monica? She *is* your sister, mammy, and she is a nun and . . .

Clara;   *(Sternly)* No – you, Isobel. And then, after the cemetery, we'll have some tea and sandwiches in the Royal Hotel for anyone who wants it and then we'll be back here to the privacy of our house.

Isobel   And supposing your other sisters want to come back . . . ?

Clara   They will all drive back to Clonmel and this house will be private.

Isobel   All right, mammy, I'll see to that.

Clara   Thank you, Isobel, and thank you, Tony. And Annabelle, from you I'd like – for my own peace of mind and so I won't be made a fool of tomorrow by people knowing more than I know – I'd like an answer to one very straightforward question.

Isobel   Mammy, don't distress yourself now . . . you should be in bed . . .

Clara   *(To Anna)* And it is this – are there any other letters under the roof of this house from that woman, similar to the one I discovered two weeks ago that your father had forgotten to hide?

Anna   *(Quietly)* No.

44

Clara	Pardon me?
Anna	I said no, there are not.
Clara	Because I am certain, Annabelle, that you know more then you pretend – I know that out there in that shop, there were things you saw and things you heard that you never told me then and you're not telling me now.
Isobel	I'm sure there are not, mammy.
Anna	*(Quietly)* There is nothing else.
Clara	I hope not – because if I find one more thing and I'm not prepared for it, you may well be held responsible for another death in this house.
Isobel	And that won't happen, mammy, because Anna said there are no more and I'm sure there aren't.
Tony	Absolutely.
Clara	Good. I'll go up then and sit with him and sprinkle some holy water on his remains and ask God again to forgive him. *(Going)*
Isobel	Do, mammy, and then we'll all go to bed because we'll need our strength for tomorrow. Come on, Tony, help mammy up the stairs. *(Going)*
Tony	No problem. And I must say, Clara, that looking at him, laid out up there, he looks like he's just fallen asleep.
Clara	He does not, Tony – he has a twisted mouth.
Tony	Oh true, but lots of people have a twisted mouth in their sleep – like Isobel here.
Isobel	I beg your pardon, Tony?
Tony	No, I mean when you're sleeping deeply, love. When you're sleeping normally, your mouth is

45

	lovely and straight, most of the time.
Isobel	Tony, would you ever shut up.
Clara	*(Turns to Anna)* I only hope you're telling me the truth – because if you're not, you won't escape the consequences. *(Goes)*
Isobel	She is, mammy. *(Goes)*
Tony	Of course she is. *(Turns to Anna. Quietly)* Talk to you again about those two words. *(Goes)*

Anna goes angrily and closes the door after them. Then:

Anna *(To herself. Bitterly)* Escape!

A tinkling piano is heard as she remembers – and the lights come up in the shop. Stephen comes to the doorway, wearing his brown overalls and now faces Anna in the living room. He is sad . . . but trying not to show it.

Stephen	Finland, did you say?
Anna	Yes, daddy.
Stephen	I don't know anyone that ever got married and went to live in Finland.
Anna	Well, David wants to.
Stephen	And do you, Anna?
Anna	Yes, if he does. You don't mind, do you, daddy?
Stephen	*(Trying)* Mind? No, no, not at all – why would I mind? It's just that . . . I thought he liked the oul shop, might like to work here with us once you got married . . . and he'd be one of our own, in the family . . . but Finland! . . . What's in Finland, Anna?

46

Anna	Seems it's the timber, daddy – and David has contacts there and he hopes to set up a partnership, start his own business.
Stephen	Making coffins?
Anna	No no, furniture – it's his father who makes the coffins.
Stephen	Oh furniture – grand. And you've somewhere to live and that?
Anna	Yes, all fixed. We've set the wedding day for June. The honeymoon in Versailles.
Stephen	Ah Versailles. Louis the Fourteenth. Grand. *(Concerned)* And have you told your mother yet?
Anna	I thought I'd tell you first.
Stephen	Oh, grand.

A customer comes into the shop, from the street, as:

Anna	And you'll be all right in the shop and everything, won't you, daddy?
Stephen	Of course I will – why wouldn't I be? *(Warmly)* Wasn't I there before you ever stood behind the counter, before I ever sat you up *on* the counter, a little girl, playing with the bull's-eyes out of the jar.
Customer	Excuse me, Stephen – do you have any packets of Brillo pads?
Stephen	*(Going to her)* Indeed I do, love – any amount of them. *(Stops, a bit lost)* Brillo . . . Brillo . . . Brillo pads . . .
Anna	*(Gently)* We're out of them, daddy – we'll have some in on Thursday.

47

Stephen	Oh, right. *(To customer)* I'm afraid we're out of them – getting them in on Thursday.
Customer	Thanks, Stephen. *(Goes)*
Stephen	Grand. *(To Anna)* Yes, Anna, that's great news altogether – and what am I thinking of . . . *(Extends his arms)* Here, congratulations – engaged, getting married and off to Finland, all in one go. *(Holds her for a moment. Then:)* You know, Isobel won't like the idea – she's been ready to come out of the traps and up the aisle for years.
Anna	I'm going to ask her to be my bridesmaid.
Stephen	Oh, grand. But I hope that Tony fella won't be asked to do anything important.
Anna	Ah, Tony's all right, and he's going to be a great footballer, going to Leeds United.
Stephen	Leeds United, my arse – Leeds Schoolboys, more likely – I've seen him playing. The less you have that fella doing at the wedding the better. But now, you better give your mother the good news. And it *is* good news, Anna, it's . . . *(Emotional now)* . . . It's really, really great, great news – *(Goes back into the shop)* and now I'd better finish what I was doing here before I get any more joyful interruptions. Yes, Finland – lovely. *Finlandia* by Sibelius. Powerful music. Ah, it must be a great country altogether. Look forward to a few holidays up there now . . . bring my skis, and why not – enter into it.

Stephen is back in the shop, closing the door, now exiting by a side door in the shop – to a storeroom, perhaps. The shop stays gently

48

illuminated while the sitting room fades, with Anna held in a
pool of light, facing us, remembering these exchanges. A spot picks
out Clara, standing at stage left. She is younger – the same age
she was when she met David. She stands, smoking.

Clara	*(Angrily)* Finland? Finland? And he's going to run that shop on his own now, is he?
Anna	He said he can.
Clara	Did he? And he can hardly remember where the door is, never mind the stock.
Anna	He *can* remember.
Clara	*(Angrily)* He *can't* remember – and you'd better face up to that. And he's only going to get a lot worse from now on – I remember the way his father went, and someday he's going to be the same, and who'll look after him then if anything happens to me? And meanwhile, this David fella can't stay in Ireland, dragging people off to Finland and a handy job laid out here for him?
Anna	David wants to specialise . . .
Clara	Oh, off you go then and specialise – I won't be here to worry about you – Dr Roberts as much as told me that only last week.
Anna	Dr Roberts? What did he tell you? Did he tell you to stop smoking those cigarettes?
Clara	Quite the opposite, if you must know. He said at this stage it didn't matter whether I stopped or not. And he's very concerned about this dizziness I get.
Anna	*(Concerned)* Dizziness? What dizziness?
Clara	Oh little you care, with your great plans. And have

	you told Isobel what you're thinking of doing?
Anna	Not yet. *(Concerned)* Mammy, what did Dr Roberts say about . . . ?
Clara	Of course you didn't tell her – you went behind her back too. Oh, that poor child coming in from a hard day's work to hear this news.

Spot out on Clara. An immediate spot on Isobel at stage right. She is back from the dentists, dressed smartly in an overcoat and carries an impressive briefcase.

Isobel	*(Angrily)* Finland?! But that means I'll have to work out there behind the counter.
Anna	You won't.
Isobel	I will because daddy won't have outsiders in, but let me tell you, I'm not going to do that, Anna, because I won't be here, I'll be gone, I'll be married and gone out of here by the time you get married.
Anna	But you're not even engaged.
Isobel	I soon will be . . . I'll be engaged this week and I'll have a ring just like yours, only bigger, and by the time June comes, I'll be married and settled somewhere, maybe in Leeds. We'll probably get married in March . . .
Anna	March . . .
Isobel	. . . or even February – Tony's been begging me for years.
Anna	Isobel . . .
Isobel	*(More angry)* . . . and at your wedding I'll be already married to him because, Anna, two can

play this game – and I don't know how you could be so cruel, to try and leave me here looking at mammy and daddy growing old and you off in Finland, married and settled and living it up – well, it's not going to happen, I'm still going to be married first out of this house, and to Tony, and I don't care what anyone says!

Isobel runs crying into the kitchen, slamming the door.

Anna   *(To the stage-right door)* You weren't saying that in the Serendipity Club, telling me to make a move and then when I made a move you suddenly go to pieces and . . .

Throughout this last speech, the stage-left door opens and Tony comes in.

Tony   Anna?

Anna turns to see him – and we are suddenly back to the present: the lights up, the shop disappears, the back wall seen again.

Anna   *(Recovering)* Ah, Tony. Has mammy gone to bed?
Tony   Not yet. She wants a glass of warm water for her heartburn.
Anna   Right, I'll get it.
Tony   No no, no problem, I can get it. Did I hear you, ya know, talking to someone again?
Anna   No no – just . . . remembering.
Tony   Oh right. It's a night for remembering, a lonely

51

	night, a sad night for memories – and, once again, you know you have my sincere . . . *(Sees Anna's look. Adjusts)* . . . sympathy. Glass of water.
Anna	She likes it just tepid – almost full glass of cold and two fingers of hot . . . boil it in the kettle and add it in.
Tony	Right. *(Going. Stops)* Oh, and Isobel asked me to ask you if you're absolutely sure that your mother won't find any more letters or anything from, ya know, Harriet.
Anna	She's not searching now, is she?
Tony	No no – she's just opening a few drawers and . . .
Anna	Jesus Christ!
Tony	But there's nothing to find, is there? Because Isobel is really afraid of a miscarriage if Clara finds something else and goes ballistic again.
Anna	*(Angrily)* No! There's nothing! She found the one letter two weeks ago, which conveniently confirmed all her jealousies and she abandoned him and drove him out of his mind the way she drives everyone either to distraction or to despair or to death – and you can go up and tell her that!
Tony	Right. *(Pause)* You haven't been thinking of yer-man, David, have you?
Anna	I beg your pardon?
Tony	Like it's a night for, ya know, thinking back and remembering, and you might be wondering . . .
Anna	*(Angrily)* No, I'm not thinking of him and I'm not remembering and I'm not wondering either. And,

	as a matter of interest, what exactly *is* there to think or to remember or to wonder about anyway?
Tony	Exactly. Nothing. All water under the bridge now. Reminds me – I'll get the water. Glass of cold and two fingers of hot.

Tony goes into kitchen, closing the door. Anna waits, then angrily slams her fist onto the table.

Anna	*(Remembering)* David!!!

A slight light change. The shop is seen in a dim light. Anna looks up and, in her memory, David is standing looking at her.

Anna	*(Sadly)* Oh David, I am so sorry.
David	*(Annoyed)* No you are not, Anna – because there is nothing to be sorry about.
Anna	*(Tearfully)* But David, I really really can't . . .
David	*(Angrily)* Yes you can, Anna, and you will.
Anna	No . . .
David	Because, Anna, our wedding is now in less than twelve hours, and because . . .
Anna	I know, but I wanted to tell you this so many times and . . .
David	*(Continuing angrily)* . . .and because in less than twelve hours all my family and all my friends will be in that church, waiting and happy and expecting . . .
Anna	But my mother!
David	And your mother will be there too because there is nothing wrong with your bloody mother . . .

53

Anna	David, she is very ill.
David	She is not very ill!
Anna	If we could just postpone it . . .
David	And I don't want to hear that word again, Anna!
Anna	Just postpone for just a few weeks until she . . .
David	*(Angrily)* And I will take a hatchet to that woman and have her either dead or alive once and for all before I will postpone anything!
Anna	David!
David	Because she is not going to do this to you and to me. Everything is arranged . . . the hotel, the reception, Versailles, Helsinki, our lives, our future . . .
Anna	I know, but . . .
David	And all this is just panic – this has come from nowhere.
Anna	*(Anxiously)* No, David, she really hasn't been well for weeks. These dizzy spells . . . I've seen them and they are so frightening and Dr Roberts wants her to have tests in hospital and mammy was a nurse, David, she knows they're serious and what's daddy going to do if . . .
David	*(Hard)* Anna, will you stop and listen to me!

Silence

David	Tonight, this is panic, it is normal, it is natural – but tomorrow you'll be grand and you'll be at the church, for our wedding, because I love you and you love me and because I know you would never ever do this to me. Am I right? Anna, am I right?

54

Anna	*(Quietly)* I'd never want to do it, David.
David	*(Gently)* And you won't. And your mother will be fine. *(Lightly)* She's been dying for years – she's hardly going to pick your wedding day to pass on! The truth is, she's panicking too – thinks that with Isobel in England, and you in Finland, she will have to work in the shop.
Anna	She can't do that, she never could, she hates serving and giving change, she was always afraid she'd be asked to.
David	And who's asking her now? I'll explain it all to her at the wedding reception – you just wait until you hear what I'm going to say in my speech – it'll be terrific, put her right at ease and no more worries. *(Lightly)* All right? OK?
Anna	*(Quietly)* Yes – I hope so.
David	Just trust me. And you'll be there tomorrow at eleven. *(Lightly)* OK, you're allowed ten minutes – at ten past eleven. And it'll be the wedding of the year – more glitzy than even Isobel's and Tony's, if that's possible!
Anna	*(Happily)* Yes, all right.
David	That's better. And here's a promise – in all our lives together, all through our married life, no matter where we are, no matter what happens, this conversation here tonight, this moment of panic will never ever be mentioned by me. It never happened. All right?
Anna	All right. Thank you, David. I'm so lucky to have you.
David	I'm the one who's lucky. Sleep well tonight.

Anna	You too.
David	Tomorrow night, we'll be lovers at Versailles.
Anna	Yes.
David	*(Kisses her)* I love you. See you in church. *(Goes through the stage-left door)*

Anna warmly watches him go, happy in this memory. The stage-right door opens and Tony comes in, carring a glass of tepid water. An immediate change of light, the shop is gone, we are back to the present day.

Tony	A watched kettle never boils – but, while I waited, I was out in your back garden, Anna – and, ya know, there's plenty of room there to extend.
Anna	Extend? Extend what?
Tony	The shop.
Anna	Extend the shop?
Tony	*(Enthusiastic)* Well, not as a shop – it's finished as a shop, the supermarket put paid to that – but remember I said I could give you some advice there: well, my assessment would be that you should consider something like, ya know, a health club.
Anna	A health club?
Tony	I've been, y'know, looking around – there's none around this area and that could be a gold mine, Anna, properly run.
Anna	Oh, I don't think so, Tony.
Tony	*(Enthusiastic)* No no – later, I might go out and check the front of the house for prospective car-parking facilities . . .

56

Anna	Tony . . .
Tony	. . . and planning permission won't be difficult because you already have a commercial outlet there . . .
Anna	Tony!
Tony	. . . and selling off that grocery stock and the fittings might get you enough capital to . . .
Anna	*(Angrily)* Tony, my father is only just dead – and that was his shop, and only days ago he was working in there!
Tony	*(Stops)* Oh yes, of course, I know, I know, and you have my sincere . . . *(Searches)* . . . whatever. *(Awkwardly)* Oh, and I've cleared this with Isobel and your mother – but I mightn't go to the Royal Hotel after the graveyard on Wednesday – I mean, ya know, I mightn't know too many people there . . . and there happens to be a Cup match on the telly about that time so I might come back here . . .
Anna	*(Quietly)* Of course.
Tony	. . . just to pass the time. And about the other thing – the health club and all, I'm only thinking of you – just said all that as, ya know, a suggestion – to give you something to think about, a new interest, give you back your self-confidence after all you've been through, after all you've lost . . . down the years. *(Awkwardly)* Bring Clara up the water.

Tony goes. Anna waits. In her head, she hears – and we hear, distantly – Sinatra singing 'Strangers in the Night', slightly distorted, slightly in echo. She picks up one of the bunches of

flowers for the funeral. Holds it like a bouquet. A light change:
the shop is lit dimly . . . and Stephen, dressed in a morning suit,
holding a hat and wearing a buttonhole – all set for the
wedding – comes in from the stage-left door. The music fades, as:

Stephen I'll have to loosen this tie – before it strangles me. *(Loosens it, now looking at Anna)* And you look lovely, Anna – lovely wedding dress, and the veil, and the gloves . . .

Anna *(Anxiously)* Daddy, how's mammy?

Stephen Much the same. She says she might phone Dr Roberts if her dizziness gets any worse . . . if she feels she might collapse again.

Anna Oh God. And what time is it?

Stephen Exactly two minutes to eleven.

Anna Two minutes to eleven? If we went off now at sixty miles an hour, we'd still be fifteen minutes late. What'll I do, daddy? Will I go? Yes? I'll just go, will I?

Stephen Fair enough. *(Fixes up his tie again. Puts on his hat)* I'll tell the driver of the limo to start his engine up again.

Anna But then supposing she does get worse and wants to phone Dr Roberts and she can't and collapses again – we can't leave her here like that, can we?

Stephen *(Returns)* Fair enough. *(Loosens his tie again, takes off his hat)*

Anna *(Distraught)* Why did Isobel and the whole lot run off like that? Is mammy still in her wedding outfit, daddy?

58

Stephen	Oh, she is – except for the hat. She took off the hat when she got back into bed.
Anna	She's back in bed? Oh my God! What'll I do, Daddy? David and everyone is waiting in the church. OK, all right, I'll go, decision made, I have to go, no choice, we'll take a chance and just go.
Stephen	Fair enough. *(Turns to go. Puts the hat on)*
Anna	Except if Dr Roberts comes, it'll be the ambulance too, maybe into hospital for tests and anything could happen . . . we can't leave her, can we?
Stephen	*(Returns. Takes the hat off)* Fair enough.
Anna	*(Angrily)* Daddy, for God's sake, you're not a pet dog waiting to be taken out for a walk – you do have an opinion. What will I do?
Stephen	What will you do?
Anna	Yes! What? For once in your life, daddy, make a decision. Will I go or will I stay. Just tell me, Yes or No, and I'll do it.
Stephen	Right. *(Pause)* Well, the way I see it is this – in life, you always have to take your chances, and that will not necessarily make everyone else happy, because by making others happy you'll often wind up making yourself unhappy, un-less . . .
Anna	Daddy, I haven't time for a speech! Just tell me! Yes or No!
Stephen	Right, in a nutshell then, you have to ask yourself are you staying or going for that reason or is there another reason and you're only using *this* reason to cover up that reason because you . . .

Anna	Is that a Yes or a No, daddy – which? *(Louder)* Which, daddy? Just say Yes or say No!
Stephen	But I can't say that, Anna.
Anna	Oh, thanks very much!
Stephen	Because I can't see what you're really thinking, deep down – so I don't know what the situation really is with you and Daniel.
Anna	*(Shocked)* You think I'm using mammy as an excuse not to go?!
Stephen	Well, nobody ever knows what's going on deep inside . . . *(Taps his head)* . . .
Anna	Daddy, I love him . . . I want to be with him, look at me, all ready to marry him – but how can I drive out in a limousine and watch an ambulance driving in at the same time?

A scream from upstairs.

| Anna | Oh God, what now? Has she collapsed again? |

The stage-left door opens and Isobel comes in. An immediate change of light – we are back to the present day. The shop disappears. But Stephen stays, as Anna holds the memory of him.

Isobel	*(Angrily)* Anna, I think you'd better come up right away.
Anna	What's wrong? Has she collapsed again?
Isobel	Again? Did she collapse before?
Anna	*(Confused)* No, no, I'm sorry . . . that was years ago . . . at my wedding.
Isobel	Your wedding? For God's sake – is that what

	you're doing down here – dreaming about your bloody wedding? Do you know what she's found up there? Three more letters from that woman.
Anna	What?
Isobel	Hidden behind the picture of 'The Laughing Cavalier'! Why the hell didn't you tell me?
Anna	I didn't know.
Isobel	Well, you'd better come up and explain – because she's now sitting on the bed beside his body, reading them, and I don't know what she's going to do.
Anna	*(Annoyed)* She wouldn't sleep with him when he was alive and now she can't be dragged from his bed.
Isobel	You read those letters and you'll see she had excellent reasons for . . .
Tony	*(Off. Shouts)* Isobel!
Isobel	Oh God, what now! *(Calls)* Coming!
Anna	And could she not wait until after the funeral to . . . ?
Isobel	*(Hard)* After the funeral will be her funeral – consider that while you're down here dreaming about your bloody wedding!

Isobel goes. A moment. Slight light change, with lights again dimly in the shop. We are back to Anna's memory. Stephen is watching her.

| **Anna** | *(Gently)* What time is it now, daddy? |
| **Stephen** | *(Looks at his watch)* Nine minutes to twelve. Don't suppose there'll be much happening now. |

Anna	No. And how's mammy?
Stephen	Says she's feeling a bit better, back on her feet, but still not a hundred per cent.
Anna	I see. If you have something to do, daddy, out there in the shop, or . . .
Stephen	No no, I'm grand, I'll stay here with you until they all come back from the church – give you a bit of support. Wait! Here's someone now.

The sound of a door closing and now Tony comes in the stage-left door. He looks shattered. He is in a morning suit, with a carnation buttonhole, back from the wedding. He carries hymn books, leaflets and some abandoned bouquets of flowers, all in a plastic bag.

Tony	Jaysus, Anna, where were you? It's bleeding pandemonium down there, all roaring and crying – it's like the losers' dressing room after the Wembley Cup final.
Anna	Did . . . did they not get my call to the presbytery? I phoned the presbytery and told . . .
Tony	Oh they got that all right – they're all on their way back. I'm just ahead of the posse.
Anna	And David, is David coming too?
Tony	Oh no. He said I was to give you this. *(A small ring-box)*
Anna	The ring? No, no, we're just postponing. I said in my phone call . . .
Tony	No, he was, ya know, very determined. He took me aside, and he was terrible annoyed, his face right up to mine, and he said that I was to tell

	you that he, ya know, couldn't believe that you'd done this to him in front of all his, ya know . . .
Anna;	*(Anxiously)* But I explained everything on the phone to the man who . . .
Stephen	*(Gently)* Calm down now, Anna.
Tony	*(To Stephen)* Hello, Mr Sullivan – all hell's breaking loose down there.
Stephen	*(Patiently)* So I gather.
Tony	You should be glad you weren't there – I mean, you should have been there, but only if you were there with Anna here but not there like I was there.
Stephen	Have you been drinking, Tony?
Tony	Oh we all have. Jaysus, you'd have to be drinking now.
Anna	Tony, did David not understand my message that I would explain everything to him . . . as soon as . . . *('I had a chance to talk to him' is implied)*
Tony	Well, Anna, to be honest, he sorta said you were not to come near him ever again and that he'd warned you . . .
Anna	What?
Tony	. . . not to do this to him and that now he'll be going to Iceland on his own . . .
Stephen	Finland.
Tony	Same place! And he said, very determined, he never wants to see you again. Not if he lives to be a hundred, he said.
Anna	Daddy . . .
Stephen	*(To soften it)* Ah now, Anna, I wouldn't mind

	that – Tony might be exaggerating.
Tony	No, no, I'm not, those were his very words.
Stephen	*(Annoyed)* All right if they were! *(To Anna)* But I'd still say they were just on the spur of the moment . . .
Tony	No no, his face was right up to mine and he was talking real slow and angry.
Stephen	*(To stop him)* All right . . .
Tony	. . . and after he finished talking, he walked away, kinda kicking the ground in a temper, and then his whole family came over and repeated the same thing all over again, except for his father, who just said that you, Anna, had a lot to answer for . . .
Stephen	All right, Tony!
Tony	. . . and that he had once liked you but not any more because he now thought you were just a selfish, brazen hussy . . .
Stephen	All right.
Tony	. . . and he hoped you'd never forget how you had ruined everybody's happiness and he hoped the day would never come that you didn't . . .
Stephen	*(Loudly)* All right, Tony, I think we have the picture!
Tony	I'm only saying what he said.
Stephen	And thanks for being so articulate! *(To Anna)* But I'd say Daniel will be different – I'd say he'll be back here once he cools down.
Tony	No, I don't think so.
Stephen	*(Loudly)* Of course he will! Why wouldn't he be!
Tony	*(Backing out of the stage-left door)* Don't blame

me – I'm only doing what I was told – and I'm sorry, Anna, for having to tell you – but a man's gotta do . . . ya know. *(Goes quickly)*

Stephen   Don't you mind all that, love. You couldn't trust that fellow with news, he was always an awful gobshite.

Anna   But daddy, David said . . .

Stephen   I'd say he got the whole message arseways – my guess is once Daniel calms down he'll see your point of view and suddenly the whole thing will be back on again and in six months' time we'll all be looking back and laughing at it all. That's what I'd say now, and I'm seldom wrong in these things. *(Goes slowly into the shop)* Ah yes, no doubt about it – all on again, the whole thing, hiring out the suits again, getting our speeches ready, getting ready to tuck into another wedding breakfast – because that Daniel is no fool: he won't pass up a chance like this. Oh, he'll be back, all right.

Stephen has gone into the shop and closed the door.

Anna   *(To herself)* Daddy?

The stage-left door opens and Clara slowly comes in. Lights change to the present day. Lights go out in the shop. Clara holds six letters in blue envelopes. She is followed by Isobel.

Clara   *(Controlled)* Isn't it a wonderful thing – you spend your whole life with one man, you feed him, you bear his children, try to make him

65

	happy, turn a blind eye whenever you can, try to think the best and then, beyond the grave, this! *(Throws the letters on the table)*
Anna	What? *(Looks at one)*
Clara	Don't be so innocent. Three more letters to put with the three I found behind 'The Laughing Cavalier'. Six in all from that . . . Harriet!
Anna	And where did you find these?
Isobel	Mammy happened to be feeling under the carpet beside the wardrobe . . .
Anna	For God's sake!
Isobel	And, Anna, you told me there were no more – and I told mammy that you'd told me, and mammy . . .
Anna	*(Angrily)* And how am I supposed to know if there are more or not?
Isobel	But mammy says he told you everything.
Anna	Well, he clearly didn't!
Isobel	Mammy says he did, and if you don't tell us now, mammy is not going to be well, and I could lose this baby if I get too upset.
Anna	But I don't know anything – there could be ten more letters, there could be hundreds more . . .
Isobel	Oh my God. *(Calls)* Tony!
Anna	I don't know – it wasn't my business to know, I wasn't married to him.
Clara	Yes, but I was – and I was the one who had to sit in here, day in and day out, on my own, looking at that wall, listening to all the skitting and the planning going on out there . . .
Anna	There was no planning . . .

Clara	And you in cahoots with him . . .
Anna	I was in cahoots with no one . . .
Clara	. . . with no concern that you were ruining my life, ruining my marriage . . .
Anna	For God's sake!
Clara	. . . the same way as, years ago, you ruined Isobel's life just as she was getting out to make something of it.
Anna	How did I ever ruin Isobel's life?
Clara	Don't act the innocent – you knew she could have had the pick of any professional man in Dublin . . .
Isobel	Mammy . . .
Clara	. . . but no, you had to provoke her into marrying that thing she's now married to . . .
Isobel	What thing? Mammy, I'm not married to a thing.
Clara	*(To Isobel)* Well, that is exactly what you called him on the telephone to me not three months ago.
Isobel	Because that was the day I found out about . . . *(Stops)* And I told you never to mention that to anyone!
Clara	*(To Anna)* And none of that would have ever happened if you hadn't provoked her into marrying him.
Anna	How did I provoke her?
Clara	By suddenly pulling the coffin-maker David O'Gorman out of the hat . . .
Anna	That had nothing . . .
Clara	. . . and convincing her that he was going to marry you . . .
Anna	He *was* going to marry me . . .

67

Clara	Oh, signs on it – and where is he?
Isobel	Mammy, that's not why I married Tony!
Anna	He's in Finland, where I should be too . . .
Isobel	I was always going to marry Tony.
Anna	*(To Clara)* . . . but you had to get one of your mysterious illnesses to stop me going.
Clara	*(To Anna)* And mustn't David O'Gorman be thanking me for that!
Anna	And you only did that because you were afraid you'd be left here with daddy . . .
Isobel	And will you both stop!
Clara	*(To Anna)* David O'Gorman must be on his knees.
Anna	Because, admit it, mammy, you couldn't abide how popular daddy was, and every chance you got, you punished him by running off to Clonmel.
Isobel	Stop it!
Clara	And wasn't I right with the letters I was finding – and now, even more letters.
Anna	Letters, letters, letters – is that all you can think of?
Clara	*(Loudly)* Yes it is – and now I want to know, once and for all, are there any more?
Anna	*(Loudly)* No, there are not – you have them all!
Isobel	*(Distraught)* And now, for God's sake, can we leave it at that because, mammy, she has said that's all there are and can we now all just get to bed and forget all this and accept, once and for all, that there are no more bloody letters to be found in this house!

Stage-left door opens. Tony comes in, delighted. He holds a blue envelope aloft.

Tony   Look – I found another letter!

He crosses to give it to Clara. But Isobel intercepts him, expertly hitting him in the stomach and chopping him as he goes down.

Isobel   *(Takes the letter)* That's all right – that's my letter. I left that upstairs – thank you, Tony.

Clara   Upstairs where? *(Snatches the letter from Isobel)*

Isobel   *(Distraught)* Upstairs anywhere! Can we just stop all this now, please – I'm not feeling well!

Tony   *(In pain)* Isobel, that hurt.

Isobel   *(To Tony)* And you're supposed to be gone to bed.

Clara   *(Looking at the letter)* As I thought – it's another one. Thank you, Tony.

Tony   *(In pain)* No problem.

Clara   *(Calmly)* And now, Anna, having said there are no more, will you kindly read this new letter and tell me if you're still saying that this Harriet woman never existed?

Anna   *(Quietly)* I never said she didn't exist. She . . . she was just a friend of his.

Clara   A friend? And this kind of talk? *(The letter)* Read it and tell me that again. *(Offers it to her)*

Anna   I don't need to read it.

Tony   *(To Isobel)* I read it – it's very . . . ho-ho, ya know.

Isobel   Shut up!

Clara   *(To Anna)* So . . . you have an explanation then, do you?

69

Anna	*(Quietly)* I promised daddy I would never tell.
Clara	I was right – cahoots.
Isobel	For God's sake, Anna, if you know, just tell us.
Anna	But I promised!
Isobel	Or do you want mammy unwell and me miscarrying. Is that what you want, is it?
Anna	*(Angrily)* All right, all right, all right! But it's a promise broken to daddy.
Clara	Go on, then. And, this time, the truth.
Anna	Then there was a Harriet that daddy knew.
Clara	I see. That he met in the shop?
Anna	No. I don't know.
Clara	Where then?
Anna	I don't know.
Clara	Then who was she?
Anna	I don't know who she was, I never met her . . . all I know is that she was a very old woman, like Margaret Rutherford or Miss Marple, that daddy was helping out.
Clara	Helping out?
Anna	I don't know everything – I only know her husband died and she used to keep telling daddy how much she missed him and daddy suggested it might help if she wrote it all down, how she felt, and she said she would, in letters, but it would be better if she could give them to someone and daddy said she could give them to him . . . and they're the letters.
Clara	*(Coldly)* I see. From this old woman?
Anna	Yes.

Clara	Whose husband's name just happened to be Stephen Sullivan?
Tony	Jaysus, that's some coincidence.
Anna	No, no, that's just on the envelope, for daddy – inside, she wrote . . .
Clara	(*Coldly*) Yes – 'My dearest darling'.
Anna	Yes – that was to her husband – her husband's real name was . . . was . . . I don't think daddy ever told me that – maybe it was John, or George, or –
Clara	(*Coldly*) Or maybe this old woman just couldn't remember what her husband's name was?
Tony	Why, did she have Alzheimer's as well?
Isobel	Tony!
Clara	As well as who, Tony?
Tony	No no, nobody.
Clara	Nobody here ever had that – Stephen was just forgetful.
Tony	I know, that's what I meant. Forgetful. Sorry. Sorry, Isobel. Sorry, Clara.
Clara	All right, Tony. (*To Anna*) And that, Annabelle, is your explanation for all these letters, is it? That they all came from an old, mysterious woman of some fantastic age who wrote passionate love letters to my husband because, somehow, she thought she was really writing to her own husband whose name she couldn't remember and who, in fact, she knew was already dead?
Anna	I don't know all the details.
Isobel	(*Disbelieving*) Oh Anna.
Clara	No no, it's possible. I could possibly believe that . . . if I was a complete idiot.

Tony	Which you're not.
Clara	Thank you, Tony. In which case, all I am left with, on this sad night, is the even sadder realisation that I have been right for years about what was happening here under my nose and out in that shop . . .
Anna	No, mammy . . .
Clara	. . . and now, by asking for an explanation, all I'm getting are more lies than I ever got before . . .
Isobel	Mammy, don't be upsetting yourself . . .
Clara	*(Sadly)* So I think it is now best if I leave it at that and not have my intelligence insulted any longer and just try to get some rest . . .
Isobel	. . . yes, and all of us . . .
Clara	*(Continuing)* . . . knowing that as long as I live on this earth, I will never discover the truth about the hidden life of that man lying dead up there who, very soon, will take all of his secrets with him to the silence of the grave.

There is a voice heard – a man's voice, clear but indistinguishable, from somewhere in the house – calling 'Hello'. All stop.

Isobel	*(Hushed)* What was that?
Clara	Quiet!
Tony	*(Hushed)* Was it outside the house?
Isobel	No, inside. He said 'Hello'.
Tony	Who did? *(Looks up fearfully towards the ceiling, where Stephen is waked)*
Clara	Anna, do you have anyone staying in this house –

72

	something else you haven't told us about?
Anna	*(Angrily)* Staying where in this house? You've been through every nook and cranny . . .
Tony	*(Suddenly)* Oh, Jesus, do you know what we forgot to do? Do you know what we never did?
Isobel	*(Panic)* What, Tony, what?
Tony	We never stuck the needles into his fingers.
Isobel	Whose fingers? What needles?
Tony	Your father – remember you said he always said he never wanted to be buried alive and we were to stick needles into . . .
Clara	Tony, will you shut up and talk sense! *(Pause. Silence)* It's gone now, whatever it was.

There are three loud knocks on the stage-left door.

Tony	Oh Jesus!
Isobel	Mammy!
Clara	Quiet, will you!
Anna	Mammy, that was definitely . . .
Clara	Quiet! *(Then)* Tony, see who that is.
Tony	What?
Clara	Open the door and see . . . or do I have to go myself?
Isobel	Just open the door, Tony. Go on!
Tony	*(Going reluctantly)* I was the one who said he only looked asleep.

Tony opens the door.

Tony	No one.

Clara	Look down the hall.
Tony	What?
Isobel	Just look down!

Tony nervously goes. Pause.

Anna	There's definitely someone . . .
Clara	*(Listening)* Quiet!
Isobel	Listen! He's talking to someone!

Voices are heard. They are indistinguishable.

Clara	Who is it?
Isobel	He's coming back.

Tony hurries in. Excited.

Tony	You won't believe this – none of you will believe this!
Isobel	What? What is it, Tony?
Tony	Firstly, Anna, remember I said I was going to check the front of the house for car-parking spaces . . . ?
Clara	What are you talking about?
Tony	Well, I must have left the front door open then . . .
Isobel	What?!
Tony	. . . so he came in and was about to go away again . . .
Clara	Who? Who was?
Tony	*(Turns. To off)* In here – we're all in here. *(To them)* Look.

74

David O'Gorman walks in tentaively.

David   Hello, Anna.

Blackout

End of Act One

ACT TWO

Scene One

Two days later. Afternoon. The sitting room, as before. The door to the shop, in the back wall, is closed. The television is on − a football match. Tony sits in front of it. He has been wearing a dark suit but the jacket is now off, tie pulled loose, shirtsleeves rolled back. He drinks a can of beer and smokes a cigarette. There are more cans in a six-pack under his chair.

Tony *(To the television)* Come on, take it down . . . good . . . now inside, cut inside . . . Don't go backwards! . . . nice . . . don't pass it! . . . oh, nice pass . . . ah, ref, studs! . . . Keep going . . . nice . . . keeper's off his line − lob him . . . watch your back! . . . opening . . . shoot! . . . Have a go! . . . Shoot! . . . Yesssss . . . *(Relaxes in despair at the shot)* Ah, ya bleeding waster . . . have to get my boots down again. *(Drinks his beer)*

A sound off stage left − the front door closing. Tony immediately puts out the cigarette, adjusts the chair, turns down the television, tries to wave away the smoke, fixes his tie, pulls down his sleeves, puts his beer aside, tries to sit casually − as Clara comes in, to be

76

followed by Isobel. It has been raining – they carry wet coats and umbrellas. Clara also carries, in a plastic bag, a basket containing a large collection of Mass and sympathy cards.

Clara	Ah, Tony.
Tony	Clara – how was it all, after?
Clara	Sad. Most of them that were up in the graveyard came to the hotel.
Tony	You didn't mind me not being at the hotel?
Clara	No no, no need for you to be going to hotels – and you were great, carrying the coffin.
Tony	An honour, Clara. And I'll say one thing for Stephen, he was really heavy – a dead weight. *(Clara looks at him. Awkwardly)* And is Isobel and Anna with you?
Clara	Isobel – we left Anna still talking. The football over?
Tony	Minutes to go – but two-one, as good as over. *(Goes towards the television reluctantly)* I'd say we're safely in the next round.
Clara	Leave it on, Tony.
Tony	Ah – I wasn't that interested. *(Very reluctantly turns it off)*
Isobel	*(Coming in)* The umbrellas, mammy?
Clara	Oh, put them in the kitchen, Isobel, into the sink.
Isobel	Did Leeds win, Toe?
Tony	Two-one, good as over. I hear there was a good crowd at the hotel.
Isobel	Yes – mostly daddy's old pals, I'd say – all very sad. *(Goes into the kitchen)*
Clara	Now – think I could do with a drop of something

	after that . . . something stronger than the tay, I think.
Tony	*(Picks up his beer)* Good idea – and it's very important to have something stronger, Clara – because it hasn't, ya know, really hit you yet – Stephen going, and all that.
Clara	*(Gets a drink)* I know, I know – the worst is yet to come.
Tony	Exactly. *(Clara looks at him. He then continues)* And we need to have a buffer zone in place when it does. I remember when my da died – Christmas morning – my sister had just given him his present, a fabulous silk tie, and he said 'Oh, that's lovely – first chance I get, I'll wear that' and dropped dead on the floor. Christmas morning, the lights on the Christmas tree, the turkey in the oven, *Top of the Pops* on the telly and my da dead on the floor. That was some Christmas, I can tell you. Luckily, we had some booze in – a buffer zone in place. *(Drinks)*
Clara	I remember that – you'd just started going out with Isobel. *(Lights a cigarette)*
Tony	That's right. But the one thing we did when we laid him out, we put that silk tie on him, to carry out his dying words – 'First chance I get, I'll wear that.' And that was the first chance . . . and the last.

Isobel comes in from the kitchen.

| **Isobel** | Freezing. |

Clara	Have a drop of this, Isobel. *(Pours a drink)*
Tony	The Christmas my father dropped dead, Isobel.
Isobel	Oh yes, dreadful – but when I met you at the funeral, remember? You were in great form, laughing your head off.
Tony	That's what I was just saying to your mother – it hadn't hit me. Like all of us here now – it hasn't hit any of us yet – Stephen gone, the shop no more. We all feel great – the funeral is over, went smoothly, no hitches – but when it does hit us, believe me, we'll need a buffer zone *(His beer)* because we'll all be in absolute bits.
Isobel	You're right, Toe. *(Drinks)* Oh, that's better.
Tony	Though I can guess who it *has* hit already – Anna. *(Drinks)*
Isobel	Well, I'm not so sure – did you notice her in the church? No tears at all. None.
Tony	Of course, it could be her mind wandering again – off on her scenic tours?
Clara	More, I think, that she had other things on her mind.
Tony	Oh, you mean like keeping an eye out for this Harriet?
Clara	*(Stops)* Pardon, Tony?
Isobel	*(Covering)* He means . . . was she there?
Clara	Well, who knows and who cares – wherever she was and whoever she is, it's all in the past and all those letters are now accounted for and burned.
Tony	And that was the right thing to do, Clara.
Clara	The only thing – and if she was there, if she was brazen enough to be there, and saw us all, then

	she knows she has a lot to answer for.
Tony	Absolutely.
Isobel	But mammy, you think that Anna was more looking out for . . . ?
Clara	Oh, no doubt – Mr David O'Gorman. But where was he? Did he give her, or any of us, more than ten words?
Tony	Just shook hands with me.
Isobel	Gave me a kiss, outside, after Mass.
Clara	Oh, and me too – but did he even look at herself?
Tony	Well, maybe . . .
Clara	*(Answering her question)* No, he did not!
Tony	*(U-turn)* That's right, no he did not.
Clara	He came over, paid his respects to our family and he's gone, back to where he came from.
Tony	Iceland.
Isobel	Finland.
Tony	Finland!!
Isobel	But I thought the night he came over to see daddy's remains . . .
Tony	Frightened the life out of us all.
Isobel	. . . I thought he might have stayed a while that night.
Clara	Oh and so did she, never saw anyone dolling themselves up so quickly.
Tony	But just up to see Stephen, said a few prayers, I noticed, then 'See you all tomorrow', and gone.
Isobel	*(A warning)* Tony!

A sound has been heard – the front door closing.

Tony	*(Quietly)* Hope it's Anna and not someone else coming to give their condolences.
Clara	Well, they shouldn't be – 'house private', we said.
Tony	And that's important for us to be house-private, because we don't know when it'll hit us and we don't want to be all seen in bits.

Anna comes in. She holds an umbrella.

Clara	Ah, Anna.
Anna	I think I got the worst of it.
Clara	That's what you get for standing talking to everyone.
Anna	A lot were our customers.
Clara	Now don't be flooding the room with that umbrella.
Anna	Right. Put it in the sink.

Anna goes into the kitchen.

Isobel	*(Quietly)* Mammy, we're going to have to bring up about what we were talking about – the shop. *(Pours herself another drink)*
Clara	Don't worry, we will. *(Declines another drink)*
Isobel	Because she still seems to think . . .
Tony	No, I think she knows – I mentioned it earlier – it just hasn't sunk in yet – you know how she is. Bit slow.
Isobel	I hope you're right. *(Then)* Mammy, I'm going up to change these clothes, they still feel damp.
Clara	Do, Isobel. Take a shower – the immersion is on.

Isobel	Great. *(Lightly)* Do you remember when we had to light a fire to heat the water to take a bath?
Clara	I fought hard to change that – and to get the central heating in. Get this house out of the Stone Age. I'll get you towels, Isobel.
Isobel	*(Calls)* Anna, do you want a shower?
Anna	*(From kitchen)* No thanks.
Clara	You're best keeping out of her way today. And Tony, all those cards from the funeral – maybe you'd put them in some kind of order for me.
Tony	Like alphabetical order?
Clara	*(Patiently)* Just tidy them, Tony.
Tony	Oh, right. Will do.
Isobel	*(Going)* You know, mammy, sometimes I can feel this little fellow kick really hard. *(Her pregnancy)*
Clara	*(Going)* Oh, another footballer.
Tony	*(Laughs)* He'd better not go to Man U – Leeds is his home and his club.
Isobel	Darling, he'll be born here now, not Leeds.
Clara	*(To Isobel)* Well, please God.
Tony	Oh right – get him into Rovers. Come on the Hoops!

Isobel and Clara go, Isobel taking her drink with her. Tony waits until they are gone, then hurries to the television and turns it on. We hear:

Commentator

        ' . . . amazing scenes here at Elland Road with Leeds conceding two goals in the dying minutes

and going out of the Cup – losing 3–2 to
Manchester United . . . '

Tony   What? No! I don't believe it! Oh, shit!

Angrily turns off the television. Lights a cigarette. Goes to the basket of sympathy cards on the table. Sits and begins to sort them. Suddenly stops on seeing one.

Tony   Oh, Jesus!

Lifts a blue envelope from the pile. Opens it and reads the card. Anna comes from the kitchen. She has a mug of tea. Tony quickly hides the card and blue envelope.

Anna   Do you want tea, Tony?

Tony   No no, I have a beer here. *(Opens a new can of beer)*

Anna   Your football over?

Tony   *(Annoyed)* Yeah, it is – well and truly over.

Anna   And do you miss it? The football – playing, and all that?

Tony   Oh yes – the roar of the crowd, the fans . . . and I'm still recognised, you know. You may have noticed, up in the graveyard, those guys standing over to the side of the grave – couldn't take their eyes off me. I could see they were wondering, 'Is it? Isn't it?' I get that a lot in Leeds too. It's nice.

Anna   Yes.

Tony   That's the good thing about funerals – you meet all your old mates. It was like that at my da's funeral too – Christmas time, everyone home, met them all.

Anna	I suppose so.
Tony	And David O'Gorman, he turned up.
Anna	Yes – nice of him to come.
Tony	Shook hands with me . . . few words about old times, how's things in Iceland, all that.
Anna	Finland.
Tony	Finland! He said his parents phoned him, told him about Stephen and he got a plane right away.
Anna	Yes.
Tony	Gone back now, is he?
Anna	I really don't know. He said he might call into the shop, when we reopen. I don't know.
Tony	Reopen?
Anna	Yes. Tomorrow, I hope. Can't lose the business.
Tony	*(Concerned)* Right. *(Pause)* I was looking at the sympathy cards.
Anna	Oh yes, so many.
Tony	*(Carefully)* And this one – look – it says 'From Harriet'.
Anna	*(Takes it)* Oh. Isn't that nice.
Tony	Look – 'I'll miss you more than words can say.'
Anna	She will too – poor old thing.
Tony	*(Unsure)* Yeah.
Anna	I suppose this will be burned too.
Tony	Which is a disgrace, I think – that they were burned.
Anna	Wasn't it you who burned them, Tony?
Tony	Oh yes, physically, because your mother told me – but I never agreed with it.
Anna	Did you not?

Tony	Absolutely not – my thinking would be, give them back to her.
Anna	Do you really think that, Tony?
Tony	Oh, absolutely – well they're hers, so to speak, if he's not around.
Anna	*(Thoughtfully)* Yes – funny, daddy once said that.
Tony	Did he? Right. *(Then, carefully)* And would you ever know who she was to give them to . . . like, what she looked like?
Anna	No – I wouldn't. But I did see some nice old ladies there today . . .
Tony	Oh right.
Anna	And I wondered, could it be one of them . . .
Tony	One little woman, in the church, small glasses and grey curls, was really crying her eyes out.
Anna	Didn't notice her – but there were so many.
Tony	Yeah. Well whoever she was, I wouldn't have burned her letters, but tried to get them back to her.
Anna	Yes.
Isobel	*(Calls from upstairs)* Tony? Are you there, Toe?
Tony	*(Calls)* Yes, Isobel – coming.
Isobel	*(Calls)* It's this shower, Tony.
Tony	*(Calls)* OK. *(To Anna)* See what this is – and maybe talk to you about that *(The card)* later. You can take one of my beers there, if you like. Buffer zone. *(Calls)* Coming, Isobel.

Tony quickly finishes his beer and goes. Anna picks up the card again, reads it. Puts it into its blue envelope. She looks at the door

85

to the shop — and remembers. Tinkling piano and a slight lighting change and now the door opens and Stephen comes from the shop. The shop beyond is in darkness. He closes the door. He wears his brown overalls and carries a cash box.

Stephen   *(Lightly)* 'Another day over and deeper in debt'. Do you remember that song, Anna? Tennessee Ernie Ford.

Anna   I do, daddy — you used to sing it.

Stephen   Sixteen tons. But doesn't apply to us . . . A good day today — no sign that that supermarket they're building will affect us in the slightest. Did I turn off the light? *(Opens the door again)* I did. *(Locks the door)* The thing is, the supermarket won't sell you three eggs or cut off two sausages or engage in a bit of chat — and that's what people want, Anna — and we're giving it to them, you and me. I'd say we're as safe as houses — our customers are like the poor, always with us. Now, put away the spondulicks. Your mother out, is she?

Anna   Gone down to the chemist before they close.

Stephen   Oh yes, the oul' heartburn was at her last night. I felt sorry for her — heard her moving around a lot. Don't think she got a wink of sleep.

Anna   Daddy, can I talk to you about this letter? *(Holds up the sympathy card in its envelope)*

Stephen   *(Not looking)* From Leeds, is it? Isobel? Nothing wrong, I hope?

Anna   No daddy, I think it's just for you. Actually, there are two — you left them on the counter when you went for your cup of tea.

Stephen	*(Turns)* What?
Anna	Both blue envelopes . . .
Stephen	Oh, blast!
Anna	It was with the other one . . . the two of them were beside the till.
Stephen	*(Suddenly angry)* Now, this is it, this is just another example of it . . . This is another bit of the brain closing down, and it's only going to get worse. Soon I won't remember where anything is . . .
Anna	. . . Daddy . . .
Stephen	*(More angry)* . . . make no mistake, this is it, Anna, this is the Alzheimer's disease . . .
Anna	. . . No, daddy . . .
Stephen	. . . or the old-timers' disease, as my poor father called it −
Anna	. . . Daddy, it is not! . . .
Stephen	*(Very angry now)* Yes it is! And we may as well call it by its right name and stop beating around the bush because this is just another proof of it and you can forget the doctors saying it's nothing − they either don't know or they won't tell you and what's the difference anyway − here, I'll take those oul' letters now . . .
Anna	Daddy, who is Harriet?
Stephen	*(Stops)* What?
Anna	I'm sorry − I read just a bit of this one, it was open and I didn't notice your name on the envelope until . . . but she signed it 'With love and kisses, Harriet' and in the letter it says she . . .
Stephen	*(Quietly)* All right, all right, I know, I know.

Anna	I didn't read the other one – and I suppose it's none of my business . . .
Stephen	*(Angrily)* And you're right, it's not! *(Then, gently)* Then again, it is. *(To himself)* Oh, blast it anyway!
Anna	*(Gently)* Daddy, what's going on? If mammy ever found anything like . . .
Stephen	*(Anxiously)* Oh don't I bloody well know it – if she sees me even smiling at some oul' wan, her suitcase is packed . . . the mercy of God you found them – if you'd gone off and got married, there'd be no one here to find these things for me and . . .
Anna	But daddy, what are these letters? There's no date, no stamp . . . and who is she – this Harriet? Did she give them to you or . . . ?
Stephen	Ah, you wouldn't know her – I hardly know her myself, to be honest.
Anna	You hardly know her but she keeps saying . . .
Stephen	I know, I know what she keeps saying! But she doesn't mean me.
Anna	She doesn't mean you? Then who, daddy?
Stephen	The thing is . . . she's an unfortunate poor devil and her husband – he must have been in his eighties . . . she looks a bit like Margaret Ruther-ford or Miss Marple on the telly – anyway he died of cancer about six months ago and it hit her hard.
Anna	And where did you meet her – here? *(The shop)*
Stephen	Ah, not at all, she was never in here. No, we used to pass each other when I'd be going down for my pint of an evening and then we got

	talking and I heard how he'd passed away and I saw the condition she was in and frail too and it was the winter and . . .
Anna	And what, daddy – she liked you, and . . . ?
Stephen	No no, all she needed was someone to listen to her going on about George – that was his name – and eventually I couldn't go out to the pub but she'd be waylaying me on the street and eventually I could take no more and I hit on a great idea: I told her to write it all down in love letters to George, to get it off her chest, and she'd feel better and I'd get to the pub for me few pints . . . so, instead of a monologue from her out in the cold, she wrote it in letters . . . and those are the result.
Anna	But daddy, if these are for her husband, George, why have you got them . . . ? And why is your name . . . ?
Stephen	Oh just on the envelope, because she gave them to me. The thing is, she said she felt better if she wasn't just piling them all up at home, but giving them to someone who was alive and never any need for me to read them or anything, and I usually don't, just open them up and leave them – and that seems to keep her happy. So what harm.
Anna	*(Convinced)* All right – but don't leave them lying around.
Stephen	I won't – I was only thinking of some place to hide those ones . . .
Anna	No, daddy, don't hide them, just burn them as soon as you get them.

Stephen	*(Stops)* Well now, Anna, I wouldn't like to do that – because I think that some day, when she's over all this, she'll get very embarrassed and she'll want them all back . . . and I'd like to be able to give them to her and let her burn them herself, if that's what she wants.
Anna	Then don't leave them lying around!
Stephen	I won't – I've great hiding places for them all.
Anna	Be careful – if mammy ever finds them . . .
Stephen	Oh, I know – there'd be ructions.

A sound off

Anna	Here she is now.
Stephen	Give the hands a wash. What's this today is?
Anna	Wednesday.
Stephen	Wednesday – gigot chops and mashed potatoes, cabbage and carrots. She does them great.

Stephen goes through the kitchen door. Anna looks again at the sympathy card.

Anna	*(To the card)* Who will you have now to write to, Harriet?

Places the card aside . . . as Tony comes in. A slight lighting change and we are back to the present day. Tony has his jacket off and is drying his hair with a towel.

Tony	That shaggin' shower! The cold is at 'red' and the hot is at 'blue' and it just comes on for no

	reason. I got soaked. Who put it in?
Anna	Oh, a friend of daddy's.
Tony	Fixed now, anyway – but Clara says she's going to have it all modified and a power-shower in there soon.
Anna	*(Coldly)* Oh yes – back in control.
Tony	*(Opens another can of beer)* Ah, it's good for her. Isobel says she can see her confidence coming back, minute by minute. *(Of the cards)* And may I say, Anna, I've no problem with, ya know, any aspects of that.
Anna	With her confidence coming back?
Tony	No, with that card – with Harriet. Now, Clara and Isobel may have a problem with it . . .
Anna	Well, tough!
Tony	Exactly – to me, it's your da helping out an old woman, for whatever reason, and I see that as both reasonable and true. *(Drinks)*
Anna	Because it *is* true.
Tony	Absolutely. What I'm saying here is, Anna, I'm on your side – I've been around, I know the score – for me, men fancying older women is OK with me . . .
Anna	But he didn't . . .
Tony	No, I know, I'm speaking generally – just saying I've no problem with that, or older men fancying younger women either, or younger men fancying younger women, or even younger men fancying younger men – oh yes, I've seen all that and no surprises, it happens – in football clubs too, the dressing rooms, the showers, you name it – not

	to me personally of course, Jaysus, no – but it's out there. And women fancying women too, no problem with that either. *(Smiles to himself)* Come to think of it, I've less problem with that than with any of the other stuff. In fact, let me say this: if you suddenly told me, here and now, that you and some other . . .
Anna	Well, I won't be suddenly telling you anything, Tony.
Tony	Oh. OK. But what I'm saying is, I'm a realist and I know what's out there and what it takes to survive out there. Which brings me nicely to those two words I gave you earlier.
Anna	What two words?
Tony	Self . . . defence.
Anna	Oh yes. You think I might be attacked by a gang of pensioners out there in the shop.
Tony	No no! But supposing, not now but any time, a gang of young bucks tried to, ya know, attack you, do you think you could, ya know . . . ?
Anna	No, I'd have no idea how to, ya know, but then I don't expect a gang of young bucks to try to, ya know, either.
Tony	And that's where you'd be wrong – because these days, no woman is safe – and looks have nothing to do with it.
Anna	Oh thanks.
Tony	No, I'm serious – just let me show you one little manoeuvre now. *(Puts his beer aside)*
Anna	I don't think so, Tony.
Tony	No, this is nothing – this is just an introductory

	demonstration I give all my enrolling students.
Anna	And I'm sure it's very interesting, but . . .
Tony	No no – there's absolutely no force involved – this one is actually designed for pensioners.
Anna	Oh thanks again.
Tony	No no, and unmarried women . . .
Anna	Like spinsters?
Tony	Exactly – who don't have a man in their lives and this will give you a basic idea – if anything happens – what you should do. It's a really simple movement – two minutes is all it takes to show you . . . you may as well see it as not see it. Right?
Anna	*(Reluctantly)* OK, all right then. Two minutes.
Tony	Two minutes max. OK, let's say, in this little improvisation, that you're standing at a bus stop . . . you're just like that, relaxed, and here's what happens. I'll do this slowly.
Anna	And no force.
Tony	Absolutely not. Slow motion. This is what your attacker does – and let's see how you react. Here I come now . . . and you suspect nothing. Here I am . . . you don't see me . . . suspect absolutely nothing and . . .

Tony has been circling in slow motion behind Anna. Now he suddenly holds her, perhaps with one hand close to her breast and one to her throat. Whatever position, it has assumed a distintly sexual hold. Anna remains motionless.

Tony   OK, Anna?

93

Anna	*(Annoyed)* Tony, what exactly is the purpose of this attack?
Tony	Doesn't matter . . . how does it feel? *(Holds her tighter)*
Anna	But what are you after? My handbag, or my money, or my bra, or . . . ?
Tony	Makes no difference – this is the hold. Now, can you escape?
Anna	No, I can't.
Tony	So without self-defence, you are helpless. Agreed?
Anna	Not quite – I could scream my head off. Which I will do, Tony, if you don't let go of me this instant.
Tony	No, don't, because I'm now going to show you how to escape.
Anna	*(Annoyed)* Just get your hands off and I'll escape by myself!
Tony	No, it's easy . . . I'll show you where to put your hand . . .
Anna	*(Angrily)* Tony, you've been drinking . . . !
Tony	No no, we'll do it in slow motion – now you reach back . . .
Anna	I have no intention . . .
Tony	No, come on, Anna . . . *(Adjusts his hold – his hand now on her breast)*
Anna	Tony, I said no!

The stage-left door opens, Isobel walks in. She wears a bathrobe. She stands watching in disbelief, as:

Tony	*(Not seeing her)* Come on . . . do it slowly . . . come on, Anna . . .
Anna	No, Tony!
Tony	Ah, come on . . .
Isobel	*(Shouts)* Tony!
Tony	*(Jumps away)* Isobel!
Isobel	*(Furious)* What the hell are you doing?
Tony	I was just . . .
Isobel	For Christ's sake, you're at it again!
Tony	No, no, I was just showing Anna . . .
Isobel	I don't believe this! *(To Anna)* Was he showing you self-defence, was he?
Tony	She asked me.
Anna	*(To Tony)* I did not!
Isobel	*(Furiously, to Anna)* Answer me, was that self-defence?
Anna	Yes, but I didn't ask him.
Isobel	*(Furiously to Tony)* Jesus Christ, Tony, after all the stuff with Jessica Davis.
Tony	This wasn't like Jessica Davis!
Isobel	Oh worse, was it?
Tony	No it wasn't and Jessica Davis never happened anyway.
Isobel	Oh and that's why we had Leeds police in to us? That's why our health club lost half its clients overnight?
Tony	It didn't! And the police left after five shaggin' minutes . . .
Isobel	And now, just as we get back on our feet . . . Jesus!
Anna	What's this about Leeds police?

95

Tony	*(To Anna)* It's nothing! *(To Isobel)* And I was doing nothing here.
Isobel	I saw you – I was looking at you.
Tony	But it was just to Anna.
Isobel	And she's not a woman?
Tony	She's only my sister-in-law!
Anna	Oh, thanks!
Isobel	And you think she wouldn't give evidence against you as quickly as Jessica Davis?
Tony	No, she wouldn't.
Isobel	Why, because she's losing her memory?
Anna	What?
Tony	No, because there's no evidence to give!
Anna	Who said I'm losing my memory?
Isobel	*(Tearfully)* Tony, this is all so unfair to me.
Anna	*(Angrily)* No, I want to know this – I'm sick and tired hearing this, and nobody . . .
Isobel	All right, you're not losing it – and daddy didn't either and our grandad didn't either . . .
Anna	I'm not daddy or grandad . . .
Isobel	*(Distraught)* . . . and meanwhile I'm trying to deal with this and with daddy dying and mammy coming back here and have a baby at the same time and trying to get out of Leeds and get fixed up into that shop before . . .
Anna	Excuse me, no one's getting fixed up in that shop.
Isobel	We've all discussed this, Anna.
Anna	No one's discussed it with me.
Isobel	The shop now belongs to mammy, and mammy wants . . .
Anna	No, the shop will be open again tomorrow . . .

Isobel	For God's sake, Anna – it's finished.
Anna	It is not, we still have our customers . . .
Isobel	*(Furiously)* Buying what? Twenty cigarettes and a box of matches! The shop is gone, Anna, and that's the end of it.
Tony	*(Loudly)* Isobel, will you for Christ's sake calm down!
Isobel	Calm down? Why should I calm down after what I just saw you doing?
Tony	Because you're pregnant and you're endangering my child by getting hysterical.
Isobel	Oh, *your* child?
Tony	And over shagging nothing, because I was doing nothing at all.
Isobel	'Nothing at all'? All right, and suppose I said this wasn't your child . . .
Tony	What?
Isobel	Supposing I said that I was *also* messing around and this child really belonged to somebody else . . .
Tony	What?
Isobel	Supposing I said I was messing with Trevor Williamson . . .
Anna	Isobel!
Isobel	. . . would that also be 'doing nothing at all'?
Tony	*(Angrily)* You better take that back this minute.
Isobel	Oh, that's different, is it?
Tony	It shagging is different, because that's my baby . . .
Isobel	So there's different rules for you?
Tony	I'm warning you – you take it back! *(Going towards Isobel)*

Anna	*(Holds Tony back)* Tony, stop, she doesn't mean it!
Tony	She does, because Trevor Williamson is one of the shaggin' dentists she works with . . .
Isobel	Maybe I was teaching him self-defence at the time.
Tony	*(Shouts)* I'm warning you!
Anna	*(Holding him)* Tony!
Isobel	Still 'nothing at all' is it?

During the last few exchanges, the stage-left door has opened and Clara has entered, leading in David O'Gorman. He is well-dressed and carries some flowers. Anna, Isobel and Tony suddenly see David and Clara . . . and stop.

Clara	*(Then, annoyed but controlled)* Excuse me for interrupting. David has come to pay his respects to the family . . . before he leaves.
David	Yes, we didn't really speak at the funeral . . . but is this a bad time?
Isobel	*(Recovering)* No no, we were just . . . just . . . just . . .
Tony	*(Recovering)* I was just demonstrating self-defence to Anna . . . and to Isobel.
Isobel	Yes – Tony instructs in the art of self-defence in Leeds.
Tony	And we were improvising a conflict-situation exercise.
David	It was very realistic.
Tony	Oh, it has to be . . . a real attack is always very . . . ya know, realistic.
David	Of course.

Clara	*(Coldly)* And none of you heard the doorbell?
Isobel	No, sorry, mammy . . .
Tony	*(Still angry)* Right. Well, I think that ends my instruction, Anna.
Anna	Oh yes. Thank you, Tony.
Tony	No problem. Any time. And if you'll excuse me, David, I'll just tidy up. *(Going)*
David	Oh certainly.
Tony	*(Hard)* And Isobel, I would like to see you privately to discuss that recent . . . revelation.
Isobel	Tony, I was just making a comparison –
Tony	Soon as possible! Upstairs! Thank you! *(Goes angrily through stage-left door)*
Clara	Now, David, some tea, perhaps, or . . . ?
David	Oh, yes, that would be nice – if you're sure I'm not . . . ?
Clara	Of course not, we are delighted to see you. Such a surprise. I'll get tea for all of us.
Isobel	*(At the drinks)* Tea, mammy?
Clara	*(Sharply)* Yes, tea, perhaps there's been enough to drink in this house. And, Isobel, your robe.
Isobel	*(Closes her robe over)* Oh excuse me.
Clara	Isobel is pregnant, you know. *(Begins to set the table)*
David	Oh congratulations.
Isobel	Thank you . . . four months to go. It will be our – Tony and mine – our third . . . we have Jason and Kate in Leeds who may be coming over soon.
David	Oh, I see.
Clara	And such lovely flowers, David, I expect these are for . . . *(Looks towards Anna)*

David	Yes, for the grave.
Clara	*(Backtracks)* Of course. *(Puts them aside)* I'll see to that. Very kind.

An awkward silence. Then:

David	And . . . and you're looking well, Mrs Sullivan.
Clara	Oh, looking well is one thing, David.
David	Yes. *(To Isobel)* And Tony still plays football for Leeds?
Clara	No . . .
Isobel	*(Quickly)* No no, he did . . . now he runs his own health club – and very successful, I'm happy to say.
Clara	And he may expand.
David	Great. And you're still in dentistry?
Isobel	Oh, yes – in a team practice now with four dentists.
David	*(Lightly)* All still pulling out the pigs' teeth?
Isobel	Pardon me?
David	No no, sorry – your dad once said that about dentists.
Isobel	Did he? Don't remember that, to be honest.
Clara	And you're still making coffins in Finland, are you, David?
David	No, never was. House furniture, custom-made, my own business now, just outside Helsinki. Last year we went into making children's wooden toys. Very popular – people tend to want to get back to things traditional.
Isobel	How interesting. *(Pause)* And did you ever get married, David?

100

David	Married? *(Beat)* Oh yes, yes I did.
Isobel	Really? Congratulations.
David	Thank you.
Clara	*(Trying)* Yes, congratulations . . . well done, David . . . great news.
Anna	*(Then)* Yes, congratulations.
David	Thanks.
Anna	I'll make the tea.
Isobel	No, I can do that.
Anna	No, you stay, I will.
Isobel	No, I'll do it.
Anna	*(Pointedly)* I'll do it. I haven't forgotten where everything is – yet!

Anna goes angrily into the kitchen.

Clara	It's a difficult time for Anna.
David	Of course, the two of them in the shop. They were a team.
Clara	Yes I always loved to see them in there.
David	Slicing the ham, cutting the cheese, exact measurement every time.
Isobel	All a thing of the past now, David.
Clara	It's all supermarkets now.
David	Yes. But you won't close, will you?
Clara	Little choice.
David	Maybe as well he's not here to see that.
Clara	And I was just saying that.
David	And he just fell . . . ?
Clara	Oh down that old trapdoor . . .
Isobel	. . . where he kept all his stores.

Clara	Probably forgot he left it open – he was for-getting everything lately . . . his father's memory went exactly the same.
David	Really?
Isobel	I remember poor grandad – never knew who anyone was, eventually.
Clara	And it's a twelve-foot drop straight down that trapdoor.
David	Good God.

Silence

David	Do you know what I'd love to do, if you don't mind: just take a last look at the old shop.
Clara	Well, of course, David. *(Gets the key)*
David	I expect it will be gone by my next visit home.
Clara	Oh without a doubt.
Tony	*(Off. Shouts angrily)* Isobel!
Isobel	And maybe I'll leave you and see what Tony wants.
David	Of course, Isobel.
Clara	But come down for tea, Isobel – and tell Tony. It will do you both good.
Isobel	All right, mammy. See you later, David.
David	OK, Isobel.
Isobel	*(Sweetly)* And really lovely to see you again. *(Goes)*
Clara	This way then, David.
David	Oh thank you.
Clara	*(Opens the door to the dark)* Everything exactly as it was. *(Goes in)*
David	Right. *(Going in)*

Clara *(From inside)* It's cold here, so close that door . . . I'll turn on the light . . . and I'll make sure this oul' trapdoor is closed. It is.

A light goes on as David closes the door behind them. At once, the kitchen door opens and Anna looks out and now enters. Clearly, she has been listening. She looks at David's flowers. A tinkling of a piano and a slight light change as she remembers.

In her memory – from stage-left door – Stephen enters. He carries some brown envelopes.

Anna Anything, daddy?

Stephen *(Sadly)* Not a thing, a few bills, nothing else.

Anna Maybe in tomorrow's post.

Stephen She's not coming back, Anna.

Anna She will, daddy – she always does.

Stephen Eleven days . . . never this long . . . the longest was three when she thought I was joking too much with old Becky McGovern . . . but never this long and not a word, nothing. If only she'd get in touch I'd even chance explaining about Harriet . . .

Anna You could write to her.

Stephen Write all that down? About Harriet and George – and have them down there in Clonmel, pulling it apart, like the Spanish Inquisition. No, I'd have to say it to her.

Anna Then try phoning her again.

Stephen And I'd get that sister of hers – Monica, the ex-nun, and her little holy voice: *(Imitates)* 'Go away – she doesn't want to talk to an adulterer.'

Anna	She didn't mean that.
Stephen	She could do with a bit of adultery herself.
Anna	Then ring later tonight – Monica always goes to bed early . . . and Maureen will answer the phone.
Stephen	She's as bad – no husband either, even more jealous – they're all the same, these unmarried ones. *(Realises)* Not that I'm including you there, Anna.
Anna	*(Lightly)* I know, daddy.
Stephen	But all those oul' wans missed their chance, all mad jealous that I got Clara. Oh this is heaven for them now, having her back on the farm – *(Imitates)* 'I warned you all along about that fella.' *(Distraught)* If only I could talk to Clara on her own.
Anna	Maybe tomorrow, she'll be back – just like she always comes back, starts cleaning the house and washing everything in sight.
Stephen	No, not now, I know it, Anna. *(Angrily)* Bloody, damn, blasted letter – how did I leave it lying there? And you warned me, Anna, when I left the two outside – blast the cursed thing.
Anna	You just forgot, daddy.
Stephen	*(Distraught)* And that's it, isn't it? I'm forgetting everything: the people in the shop, where things are, what I'm to do next – I can't remember a bloody thing any more, Anna, just like my bloody father . . .
Anna	No, daddy . . . you're just forgetful.
Stephen	It's all going – eating away my brain – and not a bloody thing I can do about it.

Anna	Everyone gets forgetful – I forget things too. And daddy, don't worry about mammy – she'll come back.
Stephen	The best woman in the world, she was.
Anna	And she still is, and when you tell her about Harriet, when you explain it, she'll understand that it was all just an act of kindness. She'll understand, you'll see. *(Then)* Daddy, there are no more letters lying around, are there, anywhere, that anyone might find?
Stephen	No.
Anna	Are you sure?
Stephen	*(Sharply)* Do you think I've forgotten that too? No, there's nothing! Now, we better get the shop opened up.
Anna	Yes, daddy. Did you finish your breakfast?
Stephen	*(Stops. Looks at her. Sadly)* Anna, I can't remember whether I did or I didn't.
Anna	I'm sure you did – I'll wash up and put everything away. Don't worry.
Stephen	Don't worry? Soon I'll have nothing to worry about, because I'll remember nothing.
Anna	*(Lightly)* 'Course you will.
Stephen	*(Sadly)* Sometimes it's not the worst way to be – remembering nothing.

Stephen has taken the key from his overalls coat pocket, opened the shop door, gone into the darkness of the shop, closed the door.

Anna	*(Calls)* Daddy, turn on the light and be careful of the trap . . .

105

Suddenly, the crash of someone falling and a frightening roar.

Anna   *(Shouts)* Daddy!

She runs to the door . . . as Clara and David come out.

Clara   Anna!
Anna   *(Backs off, embarrassed)* Mammy! Sorry.
Clara   What are you shouting for? Is something wrong?
Anna   *(Confused)* No . . . sorry, I was just . . . It's nothing – were you . . . were you looking at the shop, David?
David   Yes – lovely old memories.
Clara   Are you all right, Anna?
Anna   Yes, of course I am.
Clara   And you got everything ready in the kitchen, did you?
Anna   *(Confused)* Oh yes . . . I was going to wash up after . . .
Clara   Wash up? We were going to have some tea with David – before he goes.
Anna   Oh, yes, of course . . . sorry . . . tea.
Clara   *(Kindly)* I'll do it, Anna.
Anna   No no, I can do it.
Clara   You stay and talk with David – did you put the kettle on?
Anna   The kettle? No, sorry, I forgot.
Clara   It's all right, five minutes, David.
David   No hurry at all, Mrs Sullivan.

Clara goes to the kitchen. The door closes. An awkward silence. Then:

Anna	So I suppose that confirms everything she said about me in there?
David	Who said what about you?
Anna	Mammy, on her grand tour, about me forgetting.
David	No no, she didn't say anything at all about you in there – forgetting or otherwise. She did say how she could never manage the shop – how all she was good for was nursing.
Anna	She never qualified as a nurse.
David	She said that too. And she said she was the only girl of five in her family to get married.
Anna	Very chatty.
David	She was. And she said she was sorry to see the shop go after a hundred years in the family.
Anna	Daddy's family.
David	Yes, that's what she said. But nice to see it again. And 'the duck' is still there.
Anna	*(Lightly)* Yes, daddy loved that. And it was always 'the duck'. *(Pause)* And you're doing well?
David	Yes – though, no matter what I say, everyone here still thinks I'm making coffins.
Anna	*(Smiles)* Yes, but it's furniture.
David	To order, mostly.
Anna	And you speak Finnish all the time?
David	Yes.
Anna	Say something in Finnish.
David	Oh. *(Tenderly)* Minulla on ikava sinua. *(Translation: 'I miss you.')*
Anna	What does that mean?
David	Just . . . *(Casually)* 'Hello, how are you.'
Anna	Oh.

David	And the answer is . . . ?
Anna	What? Oh, I'm fine . . . I'm grand – for the day that's in it.
David	Yes. My condolences again.
Anna	You sound like Tony – he keeps saying that when he hasn't got anything to say.
David	Oh.
Anna	Not that you don't have anything to say.
David	No. *(A beat)* Do you, Anna?
Anna	About?
David	Anything, really.
Anna	You mean . . . how much have I forgotten?
David	I don't think you forget at all.
Anna	I do. Lots of things. It's worrying. It's in the family. *(Lightly)* But just to show that I don't forget everything – did you go to Versailles after?
David	I did.
Anna	Thought you might.
David	One for the price of two.
Anna	*(Lightly)* Yes. And do you still sing the song?
David	The song? Oh 'Strangers in the Night'? No. Did anyone ever know I had the wrong words?
Anna	I never told anyone – except daddy – I told him.
David	Bet he laughed his head off.
Anna	No, actually he agreed with you. He said you were right – that it *was* Versailles.
David	I don't believe you.
Anna	He did!
David	Well, good for him – my only supporter. *(Sadly)* He was a great man.

108

Silence. David looks at some of the sympathy cards. A slight light change as Anna remembers. We hear Sinatra singing 'Strangers in the Night' on a radio – and Stephen comes quickly from the kitchen, holding a cup of tea. Throughout, David studies the cards.

Stephen   *(Urgently)* Anna, there it is now.

Anna   What, daddy?

Stephen   On the wireless – 'Strangers in the Night'. And do you know he was right, that friend of yours – I've listened to it a few times and there's no doubt about it – it's 'Lovers at Versailles, in love forever'. And it makes sense: Versailles, Louis the Fourteenth, the city of romance. Sure what else would it be?

Anna   *(Lightly)* Daddy, it's 'Lovers at first sight'.

Stephen   First sight? Not at all – that's codology. No, it's definitely 'Versailles' – he got that absolutely right. *(Going back, triumphant)* Oh, it wasn't only making coffins that he was good at.

Stephen closes the kitchen door. Cut radio sounds. A slight light change and we are back to the present day. David has noticed Anna's giggle at Stephen's enthusiasm and now her smile at the memory.

David   What's funny?

Anna   Oh, nothing. Just thinking.

David   Not about us, then? Nothing funny in that.

Anna   No, not at all. But you got married, you say?

David   The following year, after we . . . after all that. And you?

Anna	*(Lightly)* What do you think – that I have a husband behind the wallpaper here?
David	No, but you could be married and divorced. *(Silence. Then)* Like I am.
Anna	Are you?
David	Lasted seven months and five days.
Anna	Oh. Children?
David	No.
Anna	Bet that's given you a poor impression of marriage.
David	No. Why would it?
Anna	Left at the church by one, divorced by another.
David	No, I still think marriage must be nice . . . very nice, in fact. And I never feel I was left at the . . . *(Stops as:)*

A shouted argument outside – upstairs, approaching, and on the stairs:

Tony	*(Off. Shouts angrily)* Oh we have shagging problems all right!
Isobel	*(Off. Shouts)* Because there's one rule for you and another rule for me!
Tony	*(Off)* No, because you think you can act the tart any time you shaggin' like!

Stage-left door bursts open and Tony storms in . . . followed eventually by Isobel.

Tony	*(Angrily)* Anna, excuse me, where's your mother?
Anna	In the kitchen, making tea.

110

| Tony | *(Furiously going to the kitchen)* Because she better sort out this daughter of hers or we have major problems. *(Slams the door)* |
| Isobel | *(Following him)* It's not me that needs sorting out. *(Angrily opening the door)* And don't you slam that door on me! *(Goes in, slamming the door)* |

Pause

David	What's that? Another self-defence exercise?
Anna	No no, that's not an exercise – that's a marriage.
David	Oh.
Anna	Was it like that at the end of yours?
David	No – we just stopped talking.
Anna	Just like us.
David	Not exactly – and, as I was saying, I don't think I was ever left at the church . . .
Anna	Funny, I don't remember being there.
David	Yes, all right . . . but I never really found out why you weren't there – I mean, I wouldn't consider myself 'being left' if you really *couldn't* be there, because of your mother – but, on the other hand . . . *(Stops)*
Anna	*(Prompts)* . . . on the other hand . . . ?
David	Perhaps you didn't really want to be there.
Anna	*(A beat)* You know, my father once asked me that.
David	Then he was braver than I ever was.
Anna	And I knew that's what you thought – Tony came back from the church and told me.
David	All those things I said to Tony, to say to you, they really should have been left unsaid.

Anna	So . . . even now, you don't know if I couldn't be there or didn't want to be there?
David	Didn't ask then, not asking now.
Anna	I could answer . . . just for the record.

Kitchen door opens. Tony appears, still angry, heading across to the door at stage left.

Tony	*(Shouting back)* Admit it – you never cared about Leeds United!
Isobel	*(Off)* Didn't I go there?
Tony	*(Stops)* Yes, and then you ended my football career because you wanted children.
Isobel	*(Appears)* Are you now throwing our children in my face?
Tony	Yes I am – if they *are* our children!
Isobel	Wouldn't you like to know! *(Goes back into the kitchen)*
Tony	*(Furious)* Well, Jesus, I'm not leaving on that note! *(Goes back to the kitchen)* I want shagging answers and I want them now!
Clara	*(Off)* Will you stop it and close that door!

Tony goes into the kitchen. The door is slammed.

Anna	And the answer is – I couldn't be there.
David	But you wanted to?
Anna	That's just for the record.
David	But . . . she wasn't dying.
Anna	No, she wasn't – but I didn't have a crystal ball.

112

The kitchen door opens. Clara comes out as we hear from inside:

Tony   *(Off)* I saw you with Trevor Williamson in the
             car park.

Isobel   *(Off)* You think we have sex in a car park?

Clara closes the door.

Clara   Sorry, David – tea will be slightly delayed.

David   No problem, Mrs Sullivan.

Clara   And you will have to forgive this.

David   No no, it's all right.

Clara   But the funeral has upset everyone ... and
             there has been some drink taken.

David   Of course, understandably.

Clara   So tea, hopefully, in ten minutes. Excuse me.

Clara opens the door to enter. We hear from within:

Tony   *(Off)* You say that once more and we're finished!

Door closes. Clara gone.

David   Well, I never knew you really wanted to be
             there. For the record.

Anna   And you never thought of asking, for the record?

David   And you never thought of telling?

Anna   Because I assumed you knew.

David   I didn't – I didn't have a crystal ball either.
             (Beat) And after, did you ever fancy trying
             again – I mean, if the opportunity arose, to try

	putting it all back together?
Anna	Oh no, David, absolutely not.
David	It's a good life in Finland, I'm well settled, the business is . . .
Anna	No, not a chance.
David	But why?
Anna	Why? Where do I start? After ten years, you think you still know me?
David	I don't think people really change that much . . . I don't think I have.

A crash from the kitchen.

| **Isobel** | *(Off)* I should have let her get married, go off to Finland, lose her mind if she wanted to, but at least I'd be happy. |
| **Clara** | *(Off)* Will you keep your voice down. |

Silence off

Anna	No, David, you don't know me at all – and, as you hear, soon I may not even know myself.
David	I don't believe that.
Anna	Well, it's true – because of my father and my grandfather it is quite possible . . .
David	For God's sake, anything is possible!
Anna	*(Lightly)* Although there are positives – in Finland, I'd never miss Ireland, because eventually I wouldn't know where I was.
David	Anna . . .
Anna	And we have changed – this family. Look at us,

114

everything has changed . . .

Kitchen door opens again. Tony comes out, now calmer. He is followed by Isobel and Clara.

Tony	*(Controlled)* Excuse me, David and Anna, I have been asked to apologise to both of you for ya know . . .
Anna	That's all right, Tony.
Tony	The thing is, the death of Stephen has just begun to hit us . . .
David	Understandably.
Tony	And, as a buffer zone, Isobel may have had a little too much to drink . . .
Isobel	Me?!
Tony	All right, all of us! Except you, Clara . . . and you, Anna . . . and you, David – but we needed it because we are all really in bits, as we expected to be . . . *(More angry)* . . . but on top of that . . . *(Towards Isobel)* . . . a man can only be provoked so far . . .
Isobel	*(Angrily)* Yes, a *man* can.
Clara	Isobel!
Tony	*(To Anna and David)* And I've had to listen to a certain kind of vicious talk for years.
Isobel	Yes, when you could be off teaching young ones self-defence.
Tony	*(Angrily)* OK, eveyone heard that . . . that's it – I've tried! I'm gone . . . I'm back to Leeds, see how you get on now. *(Going)*
Clara	Tony!

115

Isobel	Jessica Davis needs more instruction, does she?
Tony	*(Stops)* I'll soon find out – and I'll tell Trevor Williamson you were asking for him. *(Going)*
Isobel	Don't bother – he'll be over to see me.
Tony	*(Stops)* Will he? Just look at yourself and give me one good reason why he'd be bothered!
Clara	Tony!
Isobel	To see his baby being born – is that a good enough reason?
Clara	Isobel!
Tony	Jesus, that's it – I'm not taking any more – you've gone too far this time.
Clara	Tony . . . stop!

Tony runs at Isobel. She expertly (in a classic self-defence move) grabs his raised arm, pulls him in and knees him in the groin. He goes down in agony.

Tony	Oh Jesus!
Clara	Isobel! *(Runs to help Tony)*
Isobel	*(Repentant)* He was going to attack me.
Tony	*(In pain)* I was not, when did I ever attack you?
Clara	Get to your feet slowly, Tony.
Tony	I think she's destroyed me . . . *(Gets to his feet. Doubled over)*
Isobel	Don't blame me – you taught me how to do that.
Clara	Come on, Tony – we'll go upstairs and I'll have a look.
Tony	You're having a look at nothing.
Clara	I'm a nurse, Tony.

116

Tony	*(Going)* I don't care what you are. My privates are private.
Clara	And you come as well, Isobel – and tell Tony who the father of that baby is.
Isobel	He knows it's his.
Tony	And after what you just done to me, it'll be my shagging last.
Clara	'Deed it won't, Tony.
Isobel	*(Helping Tony)* 'Course it won't, love . . . can you stand up more? There . . . you're grand, love.
Clara	*(To David and Anna)* They'll be all right now . . . then we'll have the tea.

Tony, Isobel and Clara go. They close the stage-left door.

David	*(Lightly)* Well, I think I know a bit more about your family now.
Anna	*(Lightly)* Yes – wouldn't you be mad to come near us.
David	They all said I was mad to go to Finland, but that worked out.
Anna	*(Seriously)* This wouldn't.
David	Listen – why don't I cancel my flight so we can just talk. *(Takes a mobile phone from his pocket)*
Anna	David, no – it's nice of you, but I gave up on all of that a long time ago.
David	And so did I.
Anna	And I'm not going back.
David	Anna!
Anna	David, I often hear a lot of sounds in my head about what the future may hold, but I don't hear

wedding bells any more.

David   So, what sounds *do* you hear?

In the distance, we hear an ominous, heavy pounding sound. Very slight, but emerging.

Anna   Not sure . . . but I'd never want one of them to be the visitor's bell in a Helsinki hospital.

David   It'll never be that . . . I know it won't.

Anna   Don't be so sure – and there are other sounds I don't like either.

David   Well, let me cancel this flight anyway, give us a bit of time and maybe we'll find out. *(Dials)*

Anna   *(Hard)* No, David, just go.

The pounding sound grows louder . . . as we go to darkness.

End of Act Two, Scene One

ACT TWO

Scene Two

From the darkness, the pounding noise mixes with hard exercise music – and the lights come up.

It is six months later. The sitting room is as before. David's snow-goose carving is on the top of the television. We can see through the back wall into what was the shop, but is now a fully operational health club. A marked-out area in the back wall represents a window which is, in fact, a two-way mirror. (For production, the health club can be pre-set between Acts One and Two.)

The health club has treadmills, exercise bicycles, a ski simulator, a rowing machine and weights. There are doors to a sauna, changing room and reception room, all off. The old shop entrance is gone, with the new entrance through the reception area, off. There are about five people, of varying ages, on the exercise machines, all dressed in workout gear. Some do exercises into the mirror from their side – but we can see them as if through a window.

The door from the sitting room to the club is open, allowing the sounds out.

Establish. Then Tony comes from the stage-left door, into the sitting room. He is dressed in white trousers, white plimsolls

119

and a white T-shirt. Very confident, very efficient. With him is Sandra, an attractive reporter from the local free newspaper. She enthusiastically takes notes.

Tony	*(Loudly, over the noise)* And here it is, Sandra – this is it.
Sandra	Oh excellent.

Tony closes the door to the club. All sounds from there are now muted.

Tony	We were lucky with our planning permission – and a lot of equipment we brought over from the sale of our Leeds health club – sort of transfer to the Irish scene – and now we've plans to acquire the premises next door.
Sandra	Oh, and what was that?
Tony	Mrs Regan's cake shop, closed three weeks ago. When the supermarket opened, her rock buns hit rock-bottom.
Sandra	*(Notes this)* Oh, very good. *(Then)* Nice window.
Tony	Actually, it's a two-way mirror – we can see them, but they can't see us.
Sandra	*(Lightly)* Kinky, eh?
Tony	If you like, Sandra – but basically it allows us to monitor the club and also allows them a mirror for exercising. So, two-way benefit.
Sandra	And who ran the shop that was here?
Tony	Old Mr Sullivan and his daughter, Anna – but it was a dinosaur, losing money hand over fist. Ah, here's Isobel now.

Isobel has been coming from reception inside the club and towards the door to the sitting room, chatting with clients on her way. She looks fit and trim, dressed in a smart white outfit. She will check her hair and make-up in the mirror (thus facing us) before entering. She carries a large register.

Tony	Isobel, this is Sandra Kiernan from the *South County* newspaper.
Isobel	Oh, lovely to meet you. You're doing a piece on us?
Sandra	Oh yes, you're the success story in this area.
Isobel	Fabulous. Excuse me a sec – just a quick word, Tony. Greg Donnelly wants to switch to 3 pm tomorrow.
Tony	*(Annoyed)* Ah, not again!
Isobel	*(Looks at the register)* Maybe if we e-mail Sam Morris at his office, ask him if he'll switch to four, and we'll put Greg in at three.
Tony	Oh yes, great.
Isobel	Good. Nice to meet you, Sandra. I'll be in reception if you need me.
Sandra	Oh yes, love a chat.
Isobel	No problem. Thanks, Tony. *(Going)*
Tony	Isobel, any word on Anna?
Isobel	No, did you . . . ?
Tony	No, just leave it. I think it'll be OK.
Isobel	Great. Super.

Isobel is gone through the club, back to her reception office.

Tony	*(To Sandra)* Don't know how I'd manage

without her – wife, partner, accountant, organiser, and just great with all the clients. They love her.

Sandra   *(Taking notes)* And do you have children?

Tony   Three. The youngest is just four months old – little fellow, Simon.

Sandra   *(Noting this)* Great. And how does Isobel manage to . . . ?

Tony   That would be a problem. But luckily, we have a fabulous babysitter in her sister, Anna. She is just a treasure.

Sandra   Is this the same Anna . . . ?

Tony   . . . who worked in the shop? Right. Well, sorta dozed in a shop with no customers! But a lovely lady, never married or anything, not the most ambitious person on earth but has a great way with the kids. Simon just loves her, all the kids do.

Tony has noticed (through the window/mirror) two women coming towards the room. There is Stephanie (who is limping badly) and Rita (who is helping her). Both in their forties, in need of a fitness programme, but in all the workout gear and with Walkman headsets hanging around their necks.

Tony   Ah, excuse me, just let me buzz the nurse. *(Takes a mobile phone from his belt)*

Sandra   Is there something wrong?

Tony   No no, this lady has a weak ankle – looks like it's gone again. *(Into the mobile phone)* Nurse, soon as you can. Thank you. *(Rings off)*

Sandra   And you have a nurse on call?

Tony	Oh yes – fully qualified.

Clara comes from the stage-right (kitchen) door. She wears a nurse's white overalls.

Clara	Yes, Tony?
Tony	I think Stephanie's ankle is gone again.
Clara	Oh dear. I'll check it for her.
Tony	Clara, this is Sandra from the *South County News*. *(To Sandra)* Nurse Clara, actually Isobel's mother, but fully qualified.
Clara	You're doing the article on us?
Sandra	I am indeed. And this was your house before . . . ?
Clara	Oh, indeed it was – but sure we don't know ourselves now – run off our feet. A big change, thank God. Ah, Stephanie – in the wars again.

Stephanie and Rita have entered. The club noise is heard and shut off as the door opens and is closed.

Stephanie	Thank you, Rita. Yes, Clara, it's gone again.
Rita	*(Lightly)* I told her she was too long on the treadmill, listening to Ronan Collins.
Stephanie	*(Lightly)* I was looking at you rowing – thinking if that was a real boat, you'd be in Australia by now!
Clara	I'll look after her now, Rita.
Stephanie	Thanks, Rita . . .
Rita	If you need a lift home, tell me.
Stephanie	I should be all right – but I'll let you know.
Tony	I think you've a few more minutes on the rowing, Rita.

123

Rita	*(Merrily)* Oh, Australia here I come! *(Goes)*
Clara	Come inside, Stephanie, and I'll look at that ankle.
Stephanie	Oh, and I think I left my glasses out there somewhere.
Clara	*(Helping her)* We'll get them later – get an ice pack on that first. *(To Sandra)* See you later.
Sandra	OK – cool.

Clara helps Stephanie into the stage-right room.

Sandra	*(To Tony)* Great attention – maybe I should come in for a session myself.
Tony	Of course – why not avail of our free introductory offer?
Sandra	I might do that, Tony.
Tony	Great. *(Then)* And there's another thing – off the record – you might also be interested in some self-defence classes I run privately. There's a free sample session going for that and I personally believe every woman, married or single . . .

Isobel has come quickly through the club and is suddenly in the door.

Tony	*(Surprised)* Ah, Isobel.
Isobel	Sorry, Tony. Sandra, your photographer has arrived in reception . . .
Sandra	Oh, I'll see him, tell him what we want.
Isobel	He said he just wants to do the outside now . . .
Sandra	OK – and then I'd love to get yourself and Tony into it . . .

Tony	No problem . . . just let me finish here and I'll be out to you.
Sandra	Great.
Isobel	This way, Sandra. Let you see the club. *(Leading her to the club)*
Sandra	Thanks, Isobel . . . *(Going)* . . . and Tony, I may take you up on that offer for the self-defence class. *(Goes, ahead of Isobel)*
Isobel	*(Turns to Tony)* What?!
Tony	*(Defensive)* It was her that asked did we do them!
Isobel	*(Furious)* Jesus Christ Almighty!
Tony	No, no, I . . .

Isobel angrily follows Sandra through the club. Tony anxiously watches them through the window/mirror. Anna comes in behind him, through the stage-left door, surprising him. She is smartly dressed in a trouser suit and a fashionable coat.

Anna	Tony?
Tony	*(Jumps)* Anna!
Anna	Sorry. So, Simon is asleep and Kate and Jason are watching television . . .
Tony	OK, and what's with the coat – are you going out somewhere?
Anna	*(Angrily)* Don't act the fool, Tony, you know where I'm going – my suitcase is packed, I showed you my airline ticket . . .
Tony	*(Angrily)* For Christ's sake, Anna!
Anna	I've been saying this to all of you for two months and you have all sat there ignoring me . . .

Tony	Of course we've ignored you because you don't know where you're going. You hardly know where Iceland is . . .
Anna	Finland!
Tony	Has Isobel seen you?
Anna	Seen me? She's been looking through me for weeks.
Tony	And what about us here, have you thought of that, Anna? Have you thought about the kids?
Anna	They're not my kids, Tony.
Tony	*(Angrily)* So that's it, is it? We have to let the business slide, hire someone to look after the kids and get the meals and do the cleaning so you can go off on a wild-goose chase to Finland? For God's sake, Anna, you're part of the team here.
Anna	*(Angrily)* No, I'm not part of any team – you're all out there, all your names in the brochure, your own name over the door . . .
Tony	That's because I'm famous.
Anna	. . . while I'm hidden away upstairs like a leper, talking to no one except children, sneaking down to cook meals and clean the place when the coast is clear . . .
Tony	But that's the way businesses work – everyone has different roles, some up front, some in the background . . .

Clara and Stephanie come from the kitchen. Stephanie now has an ice pack on her ankle.

Clara	Now, Stephanie, put your foot up there and I'll find your glasses.
Tony	Clara, Anna says she's going.
Clara	She's not. *(To Stephanie)* And you're sure you had them coming in?
Stephanie	I drove down, so I had to have them. *(Sitting down)*
Clara	Well, don't worry, they have to be somewhere. Is Ronan Collins over yet?
Stephanie	No, I'll get the last twenty minutes of him. *(Puts her headphones on and listens to the music)*
Tony	Clara, she says she's going.
Clara	*(Loudly to Stephanie)* Now, you're grand. *(To Anna, angrily)* Now Anna, you get that coat off and get this idea out of your head this instant . . .
Anna	No, mammy, I've been telling you this for two months . . .
Clara	Oh, I know – I heard you . . .
Anna	But you never said one word . . .
Clara	Because I know you're not going . . .
Tony	She can't go! *(Takes out his mobile phone)*
Anna	I *am* going . . .
Clara	Anna, listen here. You know nothing about this fella – there's no commitment, no ring, no marriage . . .
Anna	There doesn't have to be a marriage!
Clara	Of course there has to be a marriage!
Anna	David and I have discussed all this when . . .
Clara	And have you discussed about when you might be sick, thousands of miles from here?
Anna	I won't be sick!

127

Clara	Anna, look at our family: what happened to your father, your grandfather, and if that happens to you out there among strangers . . .
Tony	*(Into his mobile)* Isobel, listen! *(Speaks on in a whisper)*
Anna	*(To Clara)* David isn't a stranger.
Clara	Then why isn't he here?
Anna	Because I told him not to be, that this time I'd turn up, this time he could trust me.
Clara	Trust you? He was the one that ran off at your wedding.
Anna	Only because you stopped me going to him.
Tony	Quick as you can! *(Finishes on his mobile)*
Clara	Anna, if he really wanted you then, he would have let nothing stop him.
Anna	Well, he wants me now – I know he does!
Clara	*(Hard)* Does he? Or is he just feeling sorry for you?
Anna	*(Anguished)* Mammy, that's an awful thing to say!
Clara	It has to be said, because over there you'll be nothing.
Anna	I'm nothing here!
Clara	You're with your family – not in with a nation of Finns and this fly-by-night David O'Gorman.
Stephanie	*(Loudly to Clara)* He's great at doing the impersonations.
Clara	*(Angrily)* What?
Stephanie	*(Loudly)* Ronan Collins – on the radio. *(Louder)* Any sign of my glasses?
Clara	*(Loudly)* We'll look in a minute!
Tony	Here's a magazine to read while you're waiting.
Stephanie	*(Loudly)* To read without my glasses?

128

Clara	*(Loudly, angrily)* I'll look now, all right? All right?
Stephenie	*(Loudly)* Grand. *(Listens to the music)*
Clara	*(Quietly)* Anna, you have to understand that this is all only for your own good. That's why I said all that . . . that's why I've always done everything, because I knew what was best for you, for the future. I think you see that now, don't you, Anna?

Isobel comes in, angrily, from the club.

Isobel	*(Angrily)* Now Anna, is this true?
Clara	No, Isobel . . .
Isobel	It better not be, because I have no intention of letting this business go again . . .
Clara	And it won't, because . . .
Isobel	*(Continuing angrily)* And I don't think anyone needs reminding that we are working on a knife-edge here, with a loan to be repaid and a business to build . . .
Clara	*(Louder)* Isobel, are you deaf? Anna is not going, we have spoken to her and she's now staying!
Isobel	*(To Anna)* Is that right. Are you now staying?

Pause

Tony	Of course she is.
Isobel	*(Gently)* All right. That's good. Just remember one thing, Anna, if daddy hadn't died, that David fella would never have even come over.
Clara	Exactly.

Isobel	And here, we all look after each other. OK, Anna? *(Silence)* Good. You have your airline ticket, do you?
Anna	*(Quietly)* Yes.
Clara	God!
Isobel	Phone and cancel that – you may get a refund. You didn't order a taxi to the airport or anything?
Anna	No.
Isobel	Good. And just remember that you're a vital link here, Anna – we can't replace you – without you, this place simply could not function . . . and the children really need you too.
Stephanie	*(Loudly)* I think I might have left them in reception coming in.
Clara	*(Annoyed. Loudly)* One minute – I'm going to look for them now. *(To Isobel)* Her glasses.
Isobel	Oh, right. *(To Anna)* And everything here is interchangeable – we don't all have to be doing the same things.
Clara	Of course not.
Stephanie	*(Loudly)* Or maybe they're on the shelf beside the treadmill.
Clara	*(Loudly)* All right, for God's sake – I'll look now! *(To Anna)* You're grand now, Anna, just have a bit of rest there . . . and I'll make you a cup of tea in a minute. *(Goes through the club)*
Isobel	Now. Good. And Toe, I think Paddy McCabe should have his weights reduced by now.
Tony	Oh, of course he should. OK. And Anna, you just, ya know, take it easy and we'll talk all this out later. OK? Great. *(Goes into the club)*

Isobel	*(Listens)* Is that Simon crying?
Anna	I'll go.
Isobel	*(Gently stops her)* Anna, that's what I mean – we share out the jobs. I'll go. If anyone needs reception, you can see to it. And this is the right thing, Anna, for you – but also for mammy: she puts up a good front but all this has taken its toll – and you wouldn't want to be away if anything happens to her. OK? Good. *(Calls)* Coming, Simon love.

Isobel goes through the stage-left door. Anna takes off her coat, puts it aside. Sits down. Stephanie moves to the rhythm of the music in her headphones. She catches Anna's eye. Now turns down her sound and takes off her headphones.

Stephanie	*(Quietly)* They're looking for my glasses.
Anna	Oh. Good.
Stephanie	Don't often see you here – but I hear you used to work in the shop, with your father?
Anna	Yes.
Stephanie	I hear it was a grand shop.
Anna	It was.
Stephenie	*(Gently)* And do you ever see him at all these days?
Anna	Pardon me?
Stephanie	Your father – do you ever see him?
Anna	My father is dead.
Stephanie	Oh I know that – but when you look out there, do you ever think you see him?
Anna	No.

Stephanie	I do. All the time . . . the way he was when he was happy. I knew him well, when he was happy. Don't suppose he ever mentioned me. *(A beat)* Harriet.
Anna	Pardon me?
Stephanie	*(Quietly)* That's my name – Harriet.
Anna	Harriet? The letters?
Stephanie	Oh, you know about them, do you?
Anna	Yes, but . . . *('you're too young to be Harriet' is implied)*
Stephanie	Does anyone else know?
Anna	Yes, all . . . *('of the family' is implied)*
Stephanie	Oh, I was afraid of that – that's why I changed my name when I joined here – called myself Stephanie, because it's so like Stephen. *(Stops. Unsure)* But *you* don't mind meeting me now, do you?
Anna	But you're . . . Daddy said you were about eighty.
Stephanie	*(Kindly)* Ah, did he? I suppose so you wouldn't all be too worried.
Anna	And your husband – did he really die . . . ?
Stephanie	Oh, poor George. Yes, hit by a motorbike.
Anna	A motorbike?
Stephanie	And I know, I should never have bothered your father about all that because he used to worry so much about me . . . and look, I'm still here and he's gone . . . may be all my fault.
Anna	No no . . .
Stephanie	And maybe I shouldn't be here now – I don't give a damn about exercising – but I thought it would be nice to be in the old shop where he was.
Anna	Oh?

132

Stephanie	And I often see him in there, in my mind's eye, the way he used to tell me it was. *(A beat)* He used to talk a lot about you too, you know – that's why I didn't think you'd mind meeting me.
Anna	*(Carefully)* What . . . what did he say about me?
Stephanie	Well, about Daniel. He always said you should have gone. *(Gently)* And he was right – you should. And you should go now too.
Anna	*(Carefully)* Go . . . where?
Stephanie	I heard it all. I had this *(Indicating her Walkman)* turned off. And in the past few weeks with my ankle, I've heard a lot more, sitting out here. You really should go – the way I see it, you've got a second chance.
Anna	*(Then)* Well, even if I wanted to, it's too late now.
Stephanie	I could drive you to the airport.
Anna	You? You can't – you don't have your glasses, and your foot is . . .
Stephanie	My foot's grand. *(Takes her glasses from her pocket)* And the glasses was just to occupy them, so I could maybe get to talk to you. *(Pause)* I heard so much about you from him, I feel I know you well. *(A beat)* So is it . . . Yes or No?
Anna	*(Remains)* And all those letters you wrote – were they really to your husband or . . . ?
Stephanie	George? But poor George was dead. Oh, I see – no, don't worry, the ones from your father to me are as safe as houses.
Anna	From my father to you?
Stephanie	Oh yes – lovely ones. Much more discreet than my ones to him. I suppose we both saw it as a

133

second chance, your father and me. And I'm glad we had what we had, no regrets at all, and we hurt no one – and it gave me something after George and, I think, gave your father something too. Made him happy. I hope.

Anna *(Pause. Then, quietly)* And where's your car?

Stephanie Out in your new car park.

Anna *(Pause)* The problem is . . . I don't know what's going to happen to me . . . and I don't think I'm all that well.

Stephanie *(Directly)* Anna, none of us is well . . . but the great thing about being alive at all, is that you can still give everything a chance . . . be it a first chance or a second chance. Your father used to say that. *(Beat)* And he liked this Daniel of yours. Said he once carved him a lovely snow goose.

Anna *(Amused)* Did he really call it that? 'A snow goose'?

Stephanie Of course he did. *(Beat. Quietly)* So what do you say?

Anna *(Pause)* OK.

Stephanie Good girl. I'll be just outside, a little red car and, as they used to say in the gangster pictures, I'll have the engine running.

Stephanie goes quickly – walking perfectly – through the stage-left door. Anna waits, unsure. She now looks towards the health club. The clients now seem to be exercising at a slow, rhythmic pace and the music she hears is Finlandia *by Sibelius (the slow movement – 'Hymn of Peace') – and there, amongst all the clients, strolling around, wearing his brown overalls coat, as though he were still in his shop, is Stephen.*

134

Anna watches, hearing the music, and now, deciding, puts on her coat. She comes downstage to face us as Stephen opens the health-club door and stands casually, looking at her in the sitting room.

Anna	Daddy, I'm going to Finland.
Stephen	*(Happily)* Finland – lovely. *Finlandia,* by Sibelius. Powerful music – ah, it must be a great country altogether.
Anna	To David, daddy.
Stephen	Daniel? Oh good. And is he still making the coffins?
Anna	*(Lightly)* I'll ask him for you.
Stephen	I liked him – a grand lad. Knew nothing about football, but knew his stuff about music. He was right about Versailles, you know.
Anna	*(Happily)* No, daddy, he wasn't!
Stephen	No, you'll find he was, if you listen carefully to the song.
Anna	All right, I will.
Stephen	*(Directly)* And, Anna, don't look back – there's nothing here now for you, or for me.
Anna	No, daddy.
Stephen	Good girl.

The music of Finlandia *swells as Anna looks at the room for the last time – and now sees the snow goose on the television. She takes it, and goes. Stephen watches her from the doorway, standing relaxed and contented, as the music rises louder and the lights fade, with the last remaining light on Stephen. And we go to darkness. Cross-fade* Finlandia *to 'Strangers in the Night' for the curtain call.*

THE SPIRIT OF ANNIE ROSS

This play was first presented at the Gate Theatre, Dublin, as part of the Dublin Theatre Festival, on 5 October 1999, with the following cast:

LARRY	Mark Lambert
HELEN	Lynn Cahill
WILLIAM	Fred Pearson
AISLING	Fiona Glascott
COLM	Michael Devaney
GERRY RYAN	Gerry Ryan
DIRECTOR	Ben Barnes
DESIGNER	Tom Piper
LIGHTING	Rupert Murray

for Jean

ACT ONE

Scene One

The drawing room of an old, remote three-storeyed house. The house has been unoccupied for many years, but is maintained and still furnished. Thus, under dust covers, some good solid furniture. The carpet has seen better days. Some pictures on the walls – including a large, framed photograph of a young man, circa 1920, on the back wall.

The room is on the first floor. Two high windows at back. Outside one – and close to it – a large tree. At stage left, a door from the landing, off. At stage right, a door to a dining room, off. Outside, we know, the (now-neglected) grounds are overgrown and high-walled for privacy.

It is 9.30 pm, late September. The room is dark. In the darkness, we hear a girl wistfully singing 'I Don't Want to Play in Your Yard' up to 'if you can't be good to me'. This ends in silence and is slightly eerie.

Then the stage-left door is slowly opened. Larry shines a torch into the darkness, then finds the light switch, turns on the light. He enters. He is fifty-five and formal. Seems confident. Behind him is his wife, Helen – forty-five, attractive, stylish, inclined to be fussy.

Between them, they carry sleeping bags, overnight bags, a

convector heater, a radio/recorder, torches and also Helen's cardboard box that contains a medical kit, cutlery, crockery – in short, everything that anyone could possibly need for this overnight stay.

Larry	*(Quietly)* Look, Helen, the famous drawing room.
Helen	*(Looking)* Oh, it does look spooky, doesn't it?
Larry	*(Excitedly)* It certainly does. This is it, then – our home for the night. Let's get the stuff in. *(Calls)* William? *(Annoyed)* Where the hell has he got to now?
Helen	*(Settling in)* He said he'd make sure the front door is open for the others.
Larry	More time-wasting – we should have just got the key and let ourselves in.
Helen	But isn't it his job to . . . ?
Larry	*(Unpacking)* No, it's not his job – he's only the bloody caretaker. *(Angrily)* William? *(Louder)* William!
Helen	Larry, there's plenty of time.
Larry	There's not plenty of time – we're all supposed to be locked in here by ten; it's now twenty-five-to and look at us, here on our own, nothing ready and if this goes wrong tonight . . .
Helen	It won't go wrong, and I'm sure Aisling and Colm Kearns are on their way. *(Merrily)* And, darling, I'm really sorry you ever told me William has a glass eye.
Larry	Everyone knows that.
Helen	*(Merrily)* Well, I didn't, and that's why, down there, I couldn't look him straight in the eye,

142

because I didn't know which one *was* his eye.

Larry   Well, if I had my way, he'd have two . . .

William has come in. He is in his sixties, looks older, has a slight limp. A grumpy man, he speaks with a distinctive English accent. He will now, at his own slow pace, begin to take off the dust covers, as:

Larry   *(Suddenly pleasant)* Ah, William – we found the famous drawing room.

William   *(Grumpily)* Good.

Larry   And now, I suppose we can get the dust covers off and . . .

William   *(Shouts angrily)* I'm doing it, for God's sake, look at me – I'm doing it!

Larry   So you are. Excellent. *(As the furniture is slowly revealed)* Oh, very impressive. *(Dramatically)* And when was it, William – 1933? – that Annie Ross came up from the kitchen . . .

William   *(Grumpily, as he works)* 1932.

Larry   Oh, right – 1932, that, on this night, Annie Ross came up from the kitchens . . . *(Guessing stage left)* . . . out there . . .

William   *(Indicates stage right)* . . . out there . . .

Larry   Oh, right – out *there* . . . and instead of serving Stephen Hamilton his usual nightcap, she plunged a six-inch knife into his back and then turned and ran back out through . . . *(Decides stage right)* . . . that door . . .

William   *(Indicates stage left)* . . . that door . . .

Larry   *(Annoyed)* Right – *that* door – and into the night, and nothing was heard of her until, three

	days later, her body was taken from the local quarry. *(Merrily)* And now, Helen, every year, on this very night, at exactly twenty past eleven, she returns to this very room, quietly sobbing, her lily-white hands still covered in blood . . .
Helen	*(Mock fright)* Please, darling . . .
Larry	*(Merrily)* Spooky-spooky-spooky. And William, aren't there supposed to be bloodstains here somewhere?
William	*(Of Helen)* Yeah – she's standing on them.
Helen	*(Jumps nervously away)* Oh my goodness!
Larry	*(Looking)* Oh yes! I like those. Excellent. *(With the heater)* Now, get some heat on. Can I put this plug in somewhere, William?
William	You want me to tell you where to put that plug, do you?
Larry	What? No, no – in here will be fine, thank you. *(Plugs it in)*
Helen	*(Nervously polite)* And, William, may I ask, in all your time here, caretaking, and on your own, did you ever actually . . . see anything?
William	No.
Helen	Oh, good.
William	But then I've never been here at night, have I?
Larry	*(Merrily)* Oh, the ghost only comes out at night, does she? In a union, is she – only rostered for the night shift?
Helen	Larry!
Larry	Just kidding you, William. *(Busily)* But now, time's getting on, so perhaps you'd show me where the kitchens are. *(Gives Helen his mobile phone)* And

	while we're doing that, Helen, maybe you'd try getting Colm and tell him we're in here, in case he's parked down at the gate, waiting for us.
William	That thing won't work in here.
Larry	This 'thing' works everywhere.
William	Whenever the Hamilton family comes here in the summer, none of their mobile phones ever works in here.
Larry	More spooky stuff, is it? *(To Helen)* Soon as you can, Helen – tell him to make his way up, and Aisling too if she's down there. *(Merrily to William, going)* And you know what, William? Pity you're not staying overnight with us – you make it all sound even spookier than I ever could.

Larry and William go through the stage-right door, closing it. Helen realises that she is suddenly alone. She dials. No connection. The window blind rattles a little. She notices it, nervously. She goes to the other side of the room to dial again, carefully avoiding the bloodstains. As she is checking the phone, there is a slow knock – three beats. Helen is suddenly very nervous. She goes toward the stage-right door.

Helen   *(Fearfully)* Who . . . who is there?

Helen reaches to open the stage-right door as Aisling silently comes in through the stage-left door and stands. She is nineteen, attractive, well groomed and carries an overnight bag and a sleeping bag.

Aisling   *(Then, suddenly)* Hello.

Helen screams in fright, now frightening Aisling. Both scream hysterically. Then:

Helen	*(Great relief)* Oh, Aisling, it's you . . .
Aisling	I'm so sorry . . .
Helen	*(Recovering)* No, no . . .
Aisling	I saw the light on . . .
Helen	. . . how absolutely lovely to see you.
Aisling	*(Closes the door)* And I'm really sorry I'm late, but . . .
Helen	No, we're only just here ourselves.
Aisling	I've actually been trying to get away since half-six but then old Mrs Campion walked in for a perm, without any appointment . . .
Helen	Oh dear . . .
Aisling	. . . though I didn't really mind, because her aunt once worked in here and she's full of stories . . .
Helen	And I must make an appointment with you – after all this, there could be media attention, and we will need to look our best.
Aisling	*(Merrily)* Oh, definitely – although after tonight all our hair could be sticking up forever, like hedgehogs.
Helen	Absolutely. And look, the actual, haunted room.
Aisling	God. *(Looks)* Cool.
Helen	And bloodstains.
Aisling	God.
Helen	Larry got really excited about them – I think he'll be mentioning them on the Gerry Ryan show tomorrow morning.

Aisling	And I heard him this morning and he was brilliant – I got two more pledges of twenty pounds while he was still on.
Helen	Oh, you must tell him – he so wants us to top all the other projects in cash intake . . .
Aisling	And we will!
Helen	Except that we're up against the parachute jump, the all-night fast, the 10K walk and our biggest threat, the bungee jump.
Aisling	Oh, I love the bungee jump.
Helen	*(Sternly)* Aisling, a word of advice: whatever you do, don't say that to Larry.
Aisling	Oh, sorry.
Helen	I know this weekend is all for the same great cause . . .
Aisling	Oh yes . . .
Helen and Aisling	*(Recite together)* The 'Let Us Feed the Starving Children of Africa, Asia and the Third World Weekend Project'.
Helen	Exactly – we must never forget that – it's just that Larry cannot stand the bungee-jumpers and all the attention they get, and for what? For deliberately trying to kill themselves.
Aisling	Oh, right. And where is he now?
Helen	Larry? Out with old William, getting everything organised. Oh, by the way, so you won't be embarrassed or anything, you do know that he has a glass eye, don't you?
Aisling	*(Amazed)* No. I never noticed that, honestly.
Helen	Well, he has.

Aisling	*(Slow realisation)* And was he like that when you married him – or did it happen after?
Helen	*(Annoyed)* It's not *Larry* who has the glass eye.
Aisling	Is it not?
Helen	*(Angrily)* Oh, for God's sake, Aisling – it's William, the old caretaker.
Aisling	Oh, I was thinking.
Helen	Yes. So you won't be embarrassed. *(Then)* And you're not frightened, being in here, are you – that Annie Ross might appear, or anything?
Aisling	Oh no, not in the least.
Helen	*(Bravely)* No, nor am I – not one bit, not at all.
Aisling	In fact, I'm hoping she *does* appear – I'm actually looking forward to seeing her.

Larry bursts in, angry and busy, frightening everybody.

Larry	Bastard! Anything to annoy me.
Helen	Darling, Aisling is here.
Larry	*(Brightly)* Ah, Aisling, great to see you. Helen, did you get Colm?
Helen	No, darling, I can't get out on this at all.
Larry	Course you can. *(Takes it. Dials)* Got to get things rolling . . .
Helen	Aisling heard you on Gerry Ryan, darling.
Aisling	And immediately two more people pledged twenty pounds each.
Larry	*(Dialling. No connection. Moving)* And that's what I like to hear, Aisling – because there's a lot of competition out there – especially from the bloody bungee-jumpers. What do you think

	of bungee-jumpers, Aisling – like them, do you?
Aisling	*(Sees Helen's look)* No – matter of fact, I hate them.
Larry	Good girl. Headbangers, every one of them. And if it rains tomorrow – and it's forecast – they could be washed out, so it could be up to us to meet the overall target figure.
Helen	Indeed, darling – although it's all for the same good cause:

Helen and Aisling

(Recite) The 'Let Us Feed the Starving Children of Africa, Asia and the Children . . . '

| Larry | *(Of his mobile)* Christ, no wonder I'm getting nothing – the power is down to nothing – get it on the charger. *(Gets the charger)* The last thing we need is Gerry Ryan looking for me in the morning and this happens. |

A low, sinister wailing sound is heard beyond the stage-left door. All stop.

Larry   What the hell is that?

The sound is heard again. All watch as the door slowly opens.

Aisling   Oh, Mammy!

Colm Kearns appears – he is bent low and has a dust sheet over him, with a torch under it.

Colm   *(Strange voice)* Good evening, everybody, all

149

you . . . *(takes off the sheet, straightens up)* . . . ghostbusters!

Great relief as he is revealed. He is thirty-five, good-looking, extrovert. He carries a sleeping bag and an overnight bag.

Helen	*(Relief)* Colm Kearns, I will never forgive you for this.
Colm	*(Merrily)* You should have seen your faces.
Aisling	*(Laughing)* God, my heart.
Helen	Never, ever do that again. Lovely to see you, Colm.
Colm	*(Kisses her)* And you, Helen. And Larry.
Larry	*(Merrily, shaking hands)* What an entrance. Classic. You know Aisling, from the hairdressers?
Colm	No – how are you? *(Shakes hands)*
Aisling	Pleased to meet you.
Helen	*(To Aisling)* Colm is not only one of the best teachers in his school, but the most qualified.
Larry	He has more letters after his name than in it.
Helen	And he worked absolute miracles with our two boys.
Colm	All in the past now, Helen.
Larry	You're not on that career break already?
Colm	From this month, out for a whole year.
Larry	You'll get bored – teachers always do.
Colm	I don't think so. *(Of the room)* But this place, eh?
Helen	And another floor above – bedrooms mainly.
Colm	*(Unpacking his bag)* Brilliant.
Helen	And what, in God's name, have you got there?
Colm	*(Merrily)* Ho-ho, taking no chances with the spooks tonight. *(Produces a string of garlic, hangs*

150

	it around his neck) 'Be gone, ye vampires.' And if that doesn't work . . . *(Produces a cross)* 'Depart, evil spirits.' And if all else fails, I'll fight Annie Ross on her own terms – a six-inch carving knife. *(Produces it and stabs the air)* 'Take that, ya little murderer, and that, and that!'
Helen	You are totally mad, Colm Kearns.
Colm	And, not least, champagne to kick off our wonderful night. *(Begins to open it)*
Larry	Or maybe better wait until old William goes.
Colm	Not still here, is he?
Larry	He is and it's now ten to. *(Shouts)* William?
Colm	He stopped me outside the supermarket again yesterday – has he been on to you, Aisling, about Jason Sweeney?
Aisling	About who?
Colm	The young fellow who died here.
Larry	He's already put off five people with that bloody story. *(Calls)* William!
Helen	And do you know, Colm, he has a glass eye?
Colm	Oh, yes.
Helen	Well, I didn't know that until tonight, and neither did Aisling.
Aisling	*(Merrily to Colm)* No, and as a matter of fact, I thought Helen said it was Larry that had the glass eye.
Larry	*(Turns. Seriously)* I beg your pardon, Aisling?
Helen	No, it's all right, darling, it was a simple misunderstanding.
Larry	*(Hard but controlled)* Fine. Just need to be careful, Helen, as to who – outside – might hear

151

of these 'simple misunderstandings'. *(Brightly)* Ah, William, at last – everything in order?

William has come in the stage-right door.

William   *(Dourly)* Yes, and I'll be going now.

Larry   Excellent – you know Colm Kearns?

Colm   Hello again, William.

Larry   And Aisling, from the hairdressers.

Aisling   One of our regular clients is Mrs Campion, whose aunt once worked here.

William   *(To Larry, recites, almost by rote)* So, before I go . . .

Larry   Yes, almost ten now.

William   *(Angrily picking up and continuing)* . . . so, before I go, young Mr Hamilton on the telephone from California left strict instructions that I was to lock the front door and to lock the front gate and to turn on all the alarms . . .

Larry   Yes, those are the rules I agreed with Mr Hamilton . . .

William   *(Angrily picking up)* . . . and to turn on all the alarms so you will all stay within the house tonight and, while you are here, you will not needlessly disturb any of the rooms or their furnishings . . .

Larry   We won't.

William   . . . or their furnishings and I will be here at ten o'clock in the morning to unlock the doors and turn off the alarms . . . *(Sternly to Larry)* . . . and if there is any damage within the hours of your stay here, you, Mr Synott,

	will be held solely responsible. These are Mr Hamilton's instructions to me. I presume they are clear to you, Mr Synott?
Larry	As daylight, William. And, just to check, she is due at twenty past eleven, isn't she?
William	*(Stops)* Beg your pardon?
Larry	The ghost – Annie Ross – that is her ETA, her estimated time of arrival, isn't it?
William	And it's the time young Jason Sweeney died in here.
Larry	Perfect – just so's we'll know when to expect her.
William	Right. *(Going, stops, more sinister)* And hopefully . . . I'll see you all in the morning.

William leaves, closing the door.

| Larry | *(Then calls merrily)* OK, William – just remember to keep an eye out for us. *(To all)* Keep an eye out! Get it? |

All explode with laughter. Relieved.

Helen	Larry, how could you!
Colm	You give him a hard time, Larry.
Larry	He asks for it. But now, I think, we can have our champagne reception, courtesy of Colm, after which . . .
Helen	Colm, don't pop that cork without warning us.
Larry	He won't – after which, I suggest we take our grand tour of the house . . .
Helen	Oh yes, wonderful.

Larry	. . . then back here for a late-night snack, courtesy of Helen.
Helen	*(Almost coyly)* It's nothing really.
Larry	. . . leaving us plenty of time to experience and to record that haunting at eleven-twenty . . .
Helen	*(Merrily)* Ooooh.
Larry	. . . and then our sleepover and breakfast in the morning. How does that sound to everyone?
Colm	Perfect.
Aisling	Great.
Larry	So, if all are agreed, then let the night begin. Colm – champagne?
Colm	Problem is, I've no champagne glasses.
Larry	And that's no problem – there's any amount of glasses down in the kitchen. Helen, would you like to go and get them?
Helen	*(Fearful)* Pardon, darling?
Larry	Perhaps you'd get the glasses from the kitchen.
Helen	Me?
Larry	Don't mind, do you?
Helen	No, no. Where is it, darling – the kitchen?
Larry	Out there, through the dining room next door, and then down the backstairs. But be careful on the stairs – the light is at the bottom, so you'll have to feel for it.
Helen	Right. *(Goes, stops)* Aisling, would you like to come and help?
Aisling	*(Absently)* Pardon?
Helen	*(Sharply, through fear)* Will you come and help me in the kitchen?
Aisling	Oh right, certainly.

154

Larry	*(Merrily)* Helen, you're not afraid already, are you?
Helen	Course not – but Aisling can help me down with these tea-things *(her teapot and coffee pot)* and anyway, the glasses may need a good washing.
Colm	Good point, Helen – the last person to drink out of them could have been Annie Ross herself!
Helen	You stop that now, Colm Kearns.

Aisling and Helen go.

Larry	*(Calls merrily)* And if you meet Annie, tell her she's not due for another hour and twenty minutes.
Colm	*(Calls)* Tell her to get back into her coffin.
Larry	*(Calls)* And keep the lid on.

Now, as they begin to unpack. Very relaxed.

Larry	This is going to be one great night.
Colm	Absolutely. *(Then)* And everything OK down at the building society these days, Larry?
Larry	Couldn't be better, Colm – though I may be on the move again soon.
Colm	Really?
Larry	Oh yes – and this one is really up there, Colm – all part of our drive into the UK – this is General Manager of a completely new outlet in Bromley in Kent, with the potential of opening up in central London within the year. Interviews next month and, as things stand, I am happy to say that the smart money is firmly on yours truly.

155

Colm	Bet Helen is excited?
Larry	Over the moon.

There is the sound of a door closing.

Larry	*(At the window)* Ah – and there goes old William. Look at him: hoppidy-hop, hoppidy-hop.
Colm	And you've put all the stuff about the break-in behind you now, have you?
Larry	The what, Colm?
Colm	That robbery at your building society last year.
Larry	*(Lightly)* Oh that? Yes, absolutely.
Colm	And they never . . . ?
Larry	No, they never caught the guys – but what the hell – now all in the past.
Colm	No, I meant they never got anything, did they?
Larry	Oh, not a penny. Well, the thing is that these days we know exactly what to do in these situations: how to hold our nerve, stay calm, show them that we can be just as determined as they are – and that's what we did and the buggers left empty-handed.

Helen and Aisling return. They have four champagne glasses.

Helen	*(Coming in)* Larry, I was telling Aisling about Jason Sweeney.
Colm	Champagne glasses – brilliant.
Aisling	It's really weird how he died in here, isn't it?
Larry	No, Aisling, it isn't – the fact is, Jason Sweeney

	broke in here with three other gutties to see
Aisling	Annie Ross's ghost, got a massive heart attack and dropped dead, aged nineteen. End of story. God.
Colm	William loves to say it was because he actually saw the ghost. *(Pops the champagne bottle open. Helen jumps)*
Larry	Except that the kid was probably out of his skull on drugs. *(Of the champagne)* Fill me up, Colm, I love this stuff.
Helen	*(Of Larry's glass)* Not so much, darling.
Colm	It's only bubbles, Helen.

Champagne is now poured.

Larry	So, everybody, raise your glasses to . . . to us.
Helen	*(Corrects)* And, Larry, the Starving Children of –
Larry	Yes, yes, of course, *and* the Starving Children of Africa, Asia and the Third World.
All:	To us and the Starving Children Of Africa, Asia and the Third World.

All taste. Then, without any visible cause, the picture of the young man on the back wall suddenly tilts awkwardly. All turn to look curiously at this. All dismiss it and return to the champagne. Helen appears more concerned. Then, as they relax:

Colm	Lovely. And Larry saw William going – locking the gate.
Larry	*(Mock-sinister)* So with the doors locked and gates locked, we are alone.

157

Helen	*(Merrily)* Now, Larry!
Colm	*(Merrily)* Or we hope we are!

General laughter as they sit. Helen looks again at the tilted picture. Pause. Then:

Aisling	*(Timidly)* And does anyone here think that maybe he *could* have seen something?
Larry	Who, Aisling?
Aisling	Jason Sweeney.
Larry	Jesus! Not again.
Aisling	*(Unsure)* No, I was just thinking, maybe if he *did* see something and if he wasn't prepared for it, then maybe that might have killed him.
Larry	Excuse me, Aisling, you're not saying, by any chance, that he might have seen Annie Ross, are you?
Aisling	*(Timidly)* Well, maybe he could have.
Helen	*(Nervously)* Now please, let's not get into anything like telling ghost stories . . .
Aisling	No, I'm just saying that maybe it's possible that . . .
Larry	Aisling, love, are you seriously suggesting that Annie Ross, dead, buried and decayed for nearly seventy years, walked in on Jason Sweeney, or is likely to amble in here again tonight?
Helen	*(Nervous)* For God's sake, Aisling, this isn't the Middle Ages.
Larry	That's the kind of thing that old hoppidy-hop William would believe.
Colm	True, Larry, though there are still a lot of unexplained things out there.

Larry	Ah, Colm, for God's sake!
Helen	*(Nervously angry)* Now listen, everybody, I sincerely hope we're not getting into telling ghost stories here because . . .
Larry	We're not, Helen.
Helen	*(Almost hysterical)* . . . because I told you, Larry, when you first started out on this, and I told you again this morning, that I wasn't coming here if anyone was getting into ghost stories . . .
Larry	And we're not, Helen, we're not!
Colm	No, of course we're not, and I don't subscribe to most of that stuff either, but I would have an open mind, and maybe Aisling has too.
Aisling	*(Very unsure)* Well, I just keep thinking of all the people that have ever died, all the millions and millions and millions of them, and I just think they can't all be just gone . . . nowhere, that they all must be out there . . . somewhere.
Larry	*(Amused)* Like all out there somewhere, all working out their anniversaries so they can all come back on the exact day to try to frighten the shite out of everyone?
Helen	Larry!
Larry	Helen, all I'm saying is, if they *are* out there, I hope they'd have something better to do.
Helen	*(Angrily)* All right! And now can we talk about something else?
Larry	But personally, I don't believe they *are* out there. I believe when they're gone, they're gone, and I don't ever expect to see them, in any shape or form, ever again, end of story.

Helen	Larry, could we please change the subject . . .
Larry	And, Helen, if you think about it, neither do you.
Helen	What?
Larry	Remember that evening class you did on humanism and you came home saying spirits and apparitions were all a load of superstitious rubbish?
Helen	That was only because . . .
Larry	*(Merrily, to all)* Helen goes to all these personal-advancement classes and she still thinks there's spooks out there.
Helen	And what have my classes . . . ?
Larry	Monday she's off to her pottery class, Tuesday it's rug-making, Wednesday literature appreciation, Thursday lampshade-making, Friday public speaking, and at the end of all that she's still afraid of the dark.
Colm	But Larry, people have always been afraid of . . .
Larry	And all you have to do is stop at any graveyard and listen – and all you'll hear is one big silence, because the truth is that when people die, they're gone, we bury them and that's it. So Aisling, whatever Jason Sweeney died of, it wasn't from seeing Annie Ross, no more than we'll see her or any others of the Faithful Departed here tonight, because the simple fact is, dead people are dead, they're not here, they're gone and they don't come back.
Aisling	*(Quietly)* And *I* think they do.
Larry	Then I don't think you've been listening to what I'm saying.
Aisling	*(Suddenly angry, tearful and quickly)* And I think

160

I *have* been listening and I think you're completely wrong and that they're not dead and they do come back – because my mother died early last year and I should have been with her and she was looking for me, wanting to tell me things, but I wasn't there because I went over to see my boyfriend and then she died, still asking where I was but I don't think she's gone and not coming back, I don't think I can never see her again – I think she's out there, like all the other dead people are out there, and I happen to know that they *do* come back and that's what I believe and I don't care what anyone says.

Silence. Aisling sobbing.

Larry	*(Quietly)* Jesus Christ!
Colm	*(Calmly)* OK, OK, Aisling – and you could be right. *(Pointed, to Larry)* She *could* be right.
Larry	What? *(A u-turn)* Oh right. Absolutely. Of course, you could be right.
Colm	Because, you see, Larry was just talking generally.
Larry	Exactly – it was just a general conversation.
Helen	. . . and only about Annie Ross in particular . . .
Larry	Absolutely – remember, this was Annie Ross I was referring to, not your mother. In no way am I saying that your mother, in particular, is not . . . out there . . . somewhere.
Aisling	She is!
Larry	That's right, she . . . probably is.

161

Aisling	And the reason I know she definitely is, is that every night, after she died, whenever I went to sleep, I always dreamt that she was standing there at the bottom of my bed, looking at me.
Larry	Exactly, and that happened to me too when my parents died – soon as they were gone, there they were in my dreams.
Colm	It's very common. Both my parents died when I was very young but, in my dreams, I often see them, sometimes together, sometimes singly, but always there.
Helen	*(Her turn)* Unfortunately, my parents are still alive.
Larry	*(Quietly)* Jesus.
Helen	Well, not unfortunately – I'm delighted they are, but I'm looking forward . . . I mean *when* they die, I'll be looking forward to seeing them in my dreams because I'm sure that will be . . . lovely.
Larry	Absolutely.
Colm	And who's to say it's not real?
Aisling	It is real and the reason I know it's real is that one night I was dreaming of her being at the bottom of my bed and I suddenly woke up and she was still there, standing, looking at me.
Colm	When you weren't asleep?
Aisling	Yes.
Helen	When you were awake?
Aisling	Yes.
Larry	I see. And, when you saw her standing at the bottom of your bed looking at you, you're absolutely sure that this didn't happen *before* she died?

162

Aisling	No! It was months after she died and she was standing there, alive, looking at me.
Helen	And did . . . did she say anything?
Aisling	No. She just stood there and started to whistle.
Helen	Pardon me?
Aisling	Mammy always whistled when she was happy and she was whistling that night. 'I Don't Want to Play in Your Yard'. That was the song she used to whistle.
Larry	Like it was her party piece?
Aisling	And the lovely thing is, old Mrs Campion at the hairdressers said that was the same song that Annie Ross used to sing when *she* was happy, the same as mammy used to whistle.
Larry	*(Quietly)* They could have teamed up for a duet.
Helen	*(Quickly)* And Aisling, did your mother then stop . . . whistling . . . or . . . ?
Aisling	She just faded away and I got up, quietly, not to waken my da or my brothers, and went downstairs and I had a cup of tea, and I wasn't a bit frightened – in fact, I never felt happier since she died.
Helen	Really?
Aisling	And that's the thing about the dead – once you believe in them, you can feel happy and not be frightened by them, but I think the reason Jason Sweeney died was because he wasn't expecting to see Annie, but I think she did come that night – I think she appeared like they say she appears every year, moving around or standing, watching everybody.

Colm	I heard she doesn't actually appear – you just feel that her presence has come into the room.
Aisling	Mrs Campion says that you hear her around the house first . . . moving things . . .
Helen	*(Fearfully)* Excuse me . . .
Aisling	. . . but when she comes in here she's usually gently crying . . .
Larry	*(Hard)* Oh, as well she might be – crying for the shame she brought to the Hamilton family and to this great house.
Aisling	No, Mrs Campion says she cries because Stephen Hamilton promised to marry her and then he backed out.
Larry	*(Harder)* Which, with due respect, Aisling, is a vicious lie . . .
Aisling	No, Mrs Campion says . . .
Larry	. . . seeing as how Annie Ross was only a kitchen maid and Stephen Hamilton belonged to one of the most prominent families in the whole town! *(Lighter)* However, that's not to say that it's not a good talking point for later on – but right now, everybody, at almost ten-thirty, time, I think, for the next segment of our stay here: our grand tour of the house.
Helen	Oh yes, lovely . . .
Larry	And then back here for something to eat and be all ready for whatever happens at eleven-twenty. And, Aisling, I will say this: I'm just as curious as you are, I really am – and so are all the people who sponsored us and sent in pledges, and even Gerry Ryan himself is continually

saying that there are things out there that none of us know anything about.

Helen   And the Hamiltons certainly believed . . .

Larry   Indeed they did – stayed on here for only eight years after the stabbing and then ran out of the place, off to California.

Colm   One of them, Michael, has written a book about it all, now out of print. *(At the bookcase)* It's not here, but I suspect that a copy could be somewhere in the house.

Larry   Then let's go searching . . . and exploring . . .

Helen begins to clear away the glasses enthusiastically.

Larry   *(Irritably)* Ah Helen, leave them, leave them . . .

Helen   Almost done.

Larry   And everyone, as there appears to be a shortage of light bulbs in this house, I suggest we all bring our torches.

Helen   Ours are here – and we should go together and stay close together. Aisling, you come with me.

Aisling   OK.

Larry   Helen, you go on ahead, we'll be right behind you.

Helen   *(Panic)* No, no, Larry, we are all going together.

Larry   For God's sake, Helen, we're right behind you. Go on!

Helen   If you don't come at once, we're coming back. Come on, Aisling. Shine the torch. Good girl.

Helen and Aisling are gone through stage-left door.

Larry	*(To Colm)* Good God, what did you make of that – Aisling, believing in the living dead?
Colm	Oh, that? I think she's just emotional about her mother.
Larry	She's carrying baggage – and if we're to have any credibility in this project, the last thing we need is her going on about herself and her whistling mother.
Helen	*(Off)* Larry?
Larry	*(To Colm)* But so far, we're handling it very well. Best if we both keep an eye on her – nip anything we see in the bud – that way, I think we'll have nothing to worry about. *(Calls)* On our way, ladies.

Larry and Colm go. They close the door. The room seems eerie in its emptiness. A piano gently plays 'I Don't Want to Play in Your Yard'. A distant roll of thunder . . . a soft light seems to cross the room – it could be headlights from a distant passing car perhaps – as we fade to darkness.

End of Act One, Scene One

ACT ONE

Scene Two

Lights up. It is fifteen minutes later.

> *Helen and Aisling come in the stage-left door. Aisling carries a large family photo album. Helen is now intent on setting out plates, cups, saucers, napkins and also the sandwiches, dip, and cakes she has brought for everyone. This tidying and preparation is almost an obsession. We may – or may not – notice that the picture that suddenly tilted on the back wall is now straight again.*

Helen   *(Calling back)* Don't be long, boys – tea, coffee and food in five minutes.

Aisling   I'm nearly too excited to eat now.

Helen   I suspect they are too – but let's set it out and tempt them. *(To Aisling)* No no, you sit, Aisling, I can manage. You look at the family album.

Aisling   I'm dying to see if there's a photo of Annie Ross in here . . . and maybe one of Mrs Campion's aunt as well. *(Looking)* Oh look, outside the house, when they were all here – and a horse. God.

Helen   If you see a picture of any of the bedrooms, tell me – I just loved the big double bed in the master bedroom.

Aisling	Oh, with the canopy over it?
Helen	Yes. Do you know, I always knew there was something missing in our bedroom at home, and that's it: a canopy over the bed. I'll break the news very gently to Larry – but I'll be in town first thing tomorrow, exploring the options.
Aisling	Oh look, the whole family, just below that window – and that tree was real small – look.
Helen	*(Looking)* Good Lord – the family and staff. That looks like the mother and father . . .
Aisling	Oh yeah . . .
Helen	And that's probably Michael at the back – it's his children who are now in California. And that must be Stephen Hamilton.
Aisling	God – cool.
Helen	*(Another photo)* There he is again. That's the same photo as that picture. *(Turns to look at the framed picture on the back wall. Looks again, now realising that it is no longer tilted. Concerned, but assumes that perhaps somebody righted it. Returns to the album)* And look – could that be Annie Ross?
Aisling	Oh yes, must be. She's gorgeous.
Helen	And to think, every one of them now dead and gone forever. *(Aisling looks at her. A u-turn)* Although, of course, they are all still out there . . . somewhere. *(Aisling happy. Now calmly)* I just love this – peering into the past. *(Busy again)* I didn't think I was honestly going to enjoy this evening, but I really am now.
Aisling	Me too. *(Guiltily)* But I'm really sorry for earlier, annoying everyone by blurting out about

168

	me and mammy and the dead and everything.
Helen	Aisling, you annoyed nobody – people die and we miss them.
Aisling	But blurting out about her appearing to me . . .
Helen	*(Kindly)* And who did that annoy?
Aisling	I just can't help it sometimes – everyone is always telling me that it's my big problem. Something reminds me of something – maybe something I've seen that I shouldn't have seen, or heard that I shouldn't have heard – and I just blurt it out and the awful thing is that I can hear myself blurting it out and I know I shouldn't be blurting it out but I can't stop.
Helen	*(Unsure)* Really? Well, I think it's best not to be too self-conscious about what we say.
Aisling	I suppose so.
Helen	*(Then, carefully)* However, Aisling, and before the boys come back, there is one small thing I think you should know about, and I'd really appreciate it if, during the night, with Larry here, you didn't blurt it out, so to speak.
Aisling	Oh, and I think I know what it is.
Helen	*(Lightly)* Yes, looking at you earlier, I suspected you did.
Aisling	It's about when your husband was attacked in the building society, isn't it?
Helen	What?
Aisling	*(Blurting out)* And I think that was terrible, and I know lots of people saw him getting sick with the fright and crying his eyes out . . .
Helen	Excuse me!

169

Aisling	. . . and I believe he even wet himself . . .
Helen	. . . I *beg* your pardon . . .
Aisling	. . . but I don't blame him one bit because I think having a fellow in a balaclava holding a hypodermic needle to your neck . . .
Helen	. . . would you please . . .
Aisling	. . . and screaming at you to open the safe would have anyone vomiting . . .
Helen	. . . he never vomited!
Aisling	. . . and then saying he'd come back and get you some other time . . .
Helen	*(Loudly)* Aisling!
Aisling	. . . and then he was never caught, he's still out there . . .
Helen	*(Louder)* Aisling!
Aisling	. . . I think that would drive anyone into a psychiatric hospital . . .
Helen	*(Shouts)* Aisling, will you for Christ's sake shut up and listen to me!

Silence

Helen	*(Calmer)* That is not what I was going to ask you not to blurt out.
Aisling	Is it not?
Helen	*(Controlled)* No, it is not. And anyway, that happened a long time ago, and not how you describe it either.
Aisling	*(Timidly)* Oh, right.
Helen	What I was going to ask you not to mention to Larry regards me going to your hairdressing

170

	salon on a certain day of the week.
Aisling	Oh, is it about your grey roots coming up again?
Helen	Aisling, will you just listen to me?
Aisling	Yes, sorry.
Helen	*(Carefully)* You may have noticed earlier that Larry mentioned that I go to a pottery class on a Monday night.
Aisling	Oh, yes.
Helen	And you may have immediately remembered that, on a Monday night, I usually call into you for a facial or a wash-and-blow-dry or a manicure or whatever.
Aisling	I'd forgotten that, but now that you mention it . . .
Helen	And you may have thought that was a strange preparation for making pottery?
Aisling	No, but now that . . .
Helen	Well, the explanation is, simply, on a Monday, instead of pottery, I actually visit an elderly aunt of mine, Aunt Brigid, who is very ill in hospital and who, unfortunately, is thoroughly disliked by Larry's family and consequently he would not approve of these visits – and I'd prefer if he wasn't told.
Aisling	Oh, right.
Helen	And it is only because I want to keep the old lady's spirits up by looking my best that I go to you and forego my pottery class – in short, I make that sacrifice so I can spend my evening sitting at a hospital bed, watching my dear aunt slowly die before my eyes. But you try telling that to Larry.
Aisling	*(Unsure)* Oh now you *want* me to try telling him?

171

Helen	*(Sharply)* No, I don't. What I'm saying is, I *don't* want you, under any circumstances, to try telling him about pottery or manicures or hospitals or anything because he wouldn't understand. All right?
Aisling	Oh, right. *(Then, confidentially)* But – if you don't mind me asking – if you don't go to your class to make any pottery, how do you bring home anything to show the things you're sup-posed to have made at . . .
Helen	*(Reluctantly)* Yes, yes all right! If you must know, every three weeks I go to the reject shop and buy some broken old bits and pieces. All right?
Aisling	Oh, right. And on all the other nights, do you really go . . . ?
Helen	*(Firmly)* And on all the other nights, Aisling, I go to my classes! And all I'm asking you is not to blurt out about Monday night, when I visit my aunt Maggie.
Aisling	Brigid.
Helen	Brigid! We sometimes call her Maggie for short – whom Larry dislikes so much and should it inadvertently come up, I just ask that you will support me on this.
Aisling	Oh, right, certainly. *(Determined)* Don't worry, of course I'll support you.
Helen	Good. Excellent. *(A sound. Brightly)* And here they are back, I think . . .

The stage-left door opens. Larry pushes in an old wheelchair that is loaded with books.

172

Larry	Gangway, gangway – look, ladies, look what we found.
Helen	Larry, what is that?
Larry	We presume it's the wheelchair that Stephen was confined to after Annie Ross knifed him.
Aisling	God – really?
Larry	We found it under a blanket in a back room.
Helen	How wonderful!
Larry	A nice touch if I can tell Gerry I was sitting in it at the witching hour. And look . . . *(the books)* . . . Colm is going to spend the night reading up on everything on the house – and, believe it or not, he actually found the book that Michael Hamilton wrote about the family, so forget all the rumours, we now have the facts. *(Places the books on the bookcase shelf)*
Helen	And where *is* Colm?
Larry	An excellent question, Helen – and now, remember he walked out through this door. *(Calls)* Colm Kearns, come on down.

The stage-right door opens and Colm comes merrily in. He carries a book.

Colm	*(Merrily)* Surprise, surprise!
Helen	Colm, how did you get out there?
Larry	Our intrepid explorer has been exploring the corridors . . .
Colm	. . . and they are labyrinthine – and from the bedroom above us, there is a small service staircase that goes right down to the kitchen

	beneath us . . . so I was everywhere.
Helen	*(Lightly – concerned about the picture)* Yes, I know – and you were in here when we were all out, weren't you? Adjusting the place, eh?
Larry	*(Puzzled)* Were you, Colm?
Colm	*(Puzzled)* No, I was with you. What makes you think I was in here, Helen?
Helen	What? *(Nervously)* Oh, nothing, nothing, never mind. Now, food ready here, for everybody.
Larry	Colm, did you put on the water down there?
Colm	Should be boiling by now – and Helen, this really looks delicious.
Helen	Oh, it's nothing – sandwiches here, smoked salmon or chicken-and-salad, garlic dip with crudités here, and a choice of apple tart or pecan pie or both and mints for after. And if someone would get the tea and coffee . . .
Aisling	I'll get it. *(Runs excitedly to the stage-right door)*
Larry	*(A command)* And no rush!
Aisling	Right! *(Obediently walks slowly and goes)*
Larry	We've a good twenty minutes for this excellent repast.
Colm	*(With the book)* And look, Helen, Michael Hamilton's long-lost book.
Helen	Yes, Larry told us. Well done.
Colm	By tomorrow, I'll have the full story.
Helen	Larry, will Aisling be all right down there on her own?
Larry	'Course she will – if Annie Ross appears, she can help her up with the coffee. *(Takes a bottle*

174

	of whiskey from his bag) And for us, Colm, a drop of the hard stuff.
Colm	Terrific.
Helen	*(Firmly)* No, no, Larry. *(Takes the bottle)*
Larry	Just for me and Colm.
Helen	Colm may, but not you. And you take your tablets now; it's a quarter to eleven. And a napkin there for everybody – I'll take them out of their rings for you. This one is yours, Colm.
Larry	Helen, for God's sake, we're not babies, we can look after ourselves.

Aisling comes in with a teapot and a coffee pot.

Helen	Ah, Aisling, I'll take those, thank you. Do you take sugar?
Aisling	Oh, loads, but I brought my own.
Helen	No no, I have white or brown here or sugar cubes if you like and a little tongs is there. Larry, did you take your tablets yet?
Larry	Good God – look, I'm taking them now. One. Two.
Aisling	Do you take those instead of sugar?
Larry	Something like that. *(Takes them)*
Helen	And here, Larry, some spring water, non-sparkling, to wash them down. *(Gives it to him)* Now, who's for coffee, who's for tea?
Larry	Helen, this isn't a race, this is a time to relax and quietly talk.
Helen	Colm? Tea? Coffee?
Colm	Coffee, Helen, please.

Aisling	Tea for me, please.
Helen	And I'm a tea and Larry is still a coffee – can't get him off it, but never mind. Now, everybody, come on and help yourselves.

Suddenly, the books that Larry placed on the bookcase fall to the floor. All stop to look.

Larry	Sorry. *(Goes to pick them up)* I must have left them on the edge.
Colm	*(Satisfied)* Right.

All continue. Helen, however, still concerned, looks again at the picture on the back wall, as:

Larry	I'll turn the heater down a bit now.
Helen	Not too much, darling, it'll be cold later.

All pause to see Aisling count six spoons of sugar into her cup of tea and then add half a seventh. Now all eating, all more relaxed, as:

Helen	*(Merrily)* Don't laugh, everybody, but I brought two hot-water bottles for my sleeping bag.
Colm	Poor reflection on you, Larry.
Larry	*(Merrily)* That's only her sleeping bag, Colm – no complaints elsewhere – and two fine sons to prove it.
Colm	Point taken.
Helen	I always like my bed to be heated when I get in.
Aisling	And soon you'll have a canopy over it. *(Helen*

176

	looks quickly at her. Realises) Oh Jesus – sorry.
Larry	A canopy over what?
Helen	*(Lightly to Colm)* This is going to put Larry into such a mood.
Larry	*(Merrily)* I'll decide what puts me into a mood – what is it?
Helen	*(Tentatively)* Well, I was telling Aisling that we might – might! – get a bed canopy like the one upstairs.
Colm	Oh it's wonderful, isn't it?
Larry	It's brilliant – but how's that going to put me into a mood?
Helen	Larry, you always get into a mood when I do things.
Larry	Rubbish. Don't I always praise all the things you've done to our various houses?
Helen	*(Merrily)* Just as well – if Larry had his way, we'd be living in a shoebox.
Colm	And when he gets this Bromley job, that'll be some shoebox.
Helen	Oh, you told Colm about Bromley, did you?
Larry	Yes, why not?
Helen	*(Awkwardly)* Well, hopefully.
Larry	It'll happen. No worries.
Colm	'Course it will, Larry – you're now firmly back on your feet, and fair dues to you.
Helen	*(More in hope)* Course he is.

Pause, as they eat.

| Colm | *(To Larry)* And does it ever cross your mind |

	now about those kids in the robbery, like what became of them?
Helen	*(Anxiously)* No, no . . .
Aisling	*(Supportive)* No, no . . .
Larry	Why should it cross my mind, Colm? My guess is that they are probably rotting in a basement cell somewhere for something else they did.
Helen	Most likely, I'd say.
Aisling	*(Supportive)* Yes, so would I.
Colm	Yes, but you can't be sure of that.
Larry	I don't need to be sure of it.
Colm	No, it's just that, as they threatened to get you one day, wouldn't it help to know for sure if they . . . ? *('are still around' is implied)*
Larry	*(Harder)* No, Colm, as a matter of fact, it shagging wouldn't! And the reason it wouldn't is, firstly, threats don't bother me, and secondly, I don't really give a monkey's about them one way or the other. As far as I'm concerned, what happened happened; for them it failed, for me it succeeded, it was all a long time ago, it's now over and forgotten, so why should I give a shite about them one way or the other? End of story. OK?
Colm	Fine.

Larry now tetchily indicates the teapot that Aisling has left facing him.

Larry	*(Edgy)* And Aisling, you don't mind, do you?
Aisling	Sorry?
Larry	The teapot! Just keep it that way. *(Moves it)*

178

Helen	*(To Aisling)* Don't point the teapot at Larry.
Aisling	*(To Helen)* Oh, sorry. *(To Larry)* Sorry.
Larry	No problem.
Aisling	*(To Helen)* And sorry, too, about blurting out . . .
Helen	*(Controlled)* It's all right, it's all right!

Awkward moment. Then:

Larry	And time now, I think, for a little drop of this. *(The whiskey)*
Helen	Larry!
Larry	Just a drop. Colm?
Colm	Won't say no.
Helen	Larry, you've just taken your medication . . .
Larry	Aisling, where's your glass?
Aisling	I still have my tea, thank you.
Larry	Helen won't touch it, Colm, so it's me and you. *(Pours for Colm)*
Colm	Whoa – that's plenty.
Helen	His doctor clearly told him that while he's on that medication not to . . .
Larry	It's all right, Helen, people are not really interested in my medical history . . . but listen to this: the toast is . . . to the new canopy over our bed.
Colm	*(Merrily)* Oh, very good.
All	*(Toast)* To the new canopy.
Aisling	*(Then, to Helen)* Now.
Larry	OK, Helen? And no sign of a mood, is there?
Helen	*(Reluctantly)* No.
Larry	*(Merrily)* And if, everyone, there is still any lingering doubt, let me declare publicly that I

179

	am always very proud to leave all our house furnishing, furniture and decoration in the more-than-capable hands of Helen.
Helen	*(Lightly)* I'll pretend to believe you.
Larry	It's true – everyone raves about the way our successive houses are decorated and maintained – and all those wonderful things you bring home from your classes – the paintings, the lampshades, the pottery, those little carved figurines, the rugs . . .
Colm	And do you make all these yourself, Helen?
Helen	Pardon, Colm?
Colm	*(Conversationally)* Do you make them yourself at the class – the rugs, the lampshades, the pottery?
Helen	Oh, yes.
Aisling	*(Anxiously supportive)* Oh, yes.
Larry	And you should see them, Colm – perfection. That rug we have in the lounge, you wouldn't see it in a Persian market.
Helen	Just don't look too closely at it.
Aisling	*(Supportive)* No.
Larry	And those pottery pieces, those vases and urns, they could genuinely have come from the Greek Islands.
Colm	And how long would it have taken you to make one of those, Helen?
Helen	Sorry, Colm?
Colm	One of those pieces of pottery – how long would it take you to make it?
Aisling	*(Helping)* About three weeks.
Larry	Do you make pottery as well, Aisling?

180

Aisling	Me? No, I'm just guessing.
Helen	And it's a good guess, Aisling – three weeks usually for the larger vases and urns.
Aisling	Yes – for the larger ones.
Larry	And then we have the big and small rugs, the figurines, woodcarvings, watercolours, not to mention the most beautiful hand-painted lampshades that Helen makes on a Thursday. Absolutely magnificent, those lampshades – our pride and joy.
Helen	Thank you, darling.
Larry	You're welcome, Helen. *(Then, suddenly)* Aisling, do you mind? The bloody teapot!
Aisling	Sorry, do you want some tea?
Larry	*(Angrily moves the teapot, burning his hands)* Keep it that way! OK? OK?
Aisling	Oh, sorry. Sorry.
Larry	Not to worry. *(Continuing)* And the thing is, Colm . . .
Helen	*(Suddenly)* Did anyone hear that?
Aisling	What?
Helen	Maybe it was nothing.
Colm	You all right, Helen?
Helen	Yes. Fine. Thanks, Colm. Sorry, Larry.
Larry	And the thing is, Colm, that the net result of all this is, when we have business friends over to dinner – maybe when there's a new appointment hanging in the air – what do they notice? They notice our house, they notice Helen and what she's done, they see our two boys, they see me and they don't think, 'Hey, he left school at fifteen', they think, 'This guy has created a great

	infrastructure, this guy is focused, this guy is going places.' And, Colm – with respect – I think I know why you are not. *(Drinks)*
Colm	Not what, Larry?
Larry	Face it, Colm, with your qualifications, you should be right up there. What you lack – in my estimation – is a good social infrastructure to back up your know-how.
Colm	*(Amused)* Do I?
Larry	Tell me I'm wrong if you like, but let's face it – you live with your aunt, you've got no wife, no kids, no house – OK, you may be popular . . .
Helen	*(Warmly)* Oh, he is.
Larry	But it's not enough! You need to get yourself socially positioned to make the moves when promotions, career opportunities, advancements present themselves.
Colm	Well, Larry, you could be right . . .
Larry	I *am* right.
Colm	Except that none of it applies to me.
Larry	None of what?
Colm	Promotions, career opportunities – all that stuff.
Larry	Not now, because you're on a career break.
Colm	No, at any time. Maybe it did once, but not any more. In fact, you know this one-year career break I'm on? With any luck, it's not for a year, it's for life. Between us, I've no intention of ever going back to permanent work again.
Larry	What?
Helen	You're not going to be a teacher any more?
Larry	What are you going to do instead?

Colm   Well, to answer that, let me ask you this: did any of you ever sit at a hospital bed and watch someone die?

Aisling   *(Blurting out)* Oh yes, Helen was just telling me how she sits every . . .

Helen looks at her, aghast.

Aisling   *(Recovering)* . . . how she sits . . . sits at a thing that looks like a hospital bed, making pottery every Monday, but I don't because it takes three weeks for the larger ones . . . and I was saying how I *should* have been at my mother's bed when *she* was dying, but I was over with my boyfriend, Keith – so no, I don't think any of us has ever sat and watched someone die in a hospital bed, have we?

Helen   *(Annoyed)* No, we haven't!

Colm   Well, I did. Not long ago, I sat at a hospital bed and I watched myself die.

Aisling   You died?

Colm   No, in the end I didn't die . . . but on that bed – where I had undergone a medical for life insurance, and with all my degrees and qualifications under my belt – I looked at myself in the reflection of the window and thought of what that young doctor had just told me: they had found something, it might not be serious, but if it was, I'd be dead in four months.

Helen   Oh, Colm.

Aisling   Oh God, I think if I heard I had something that was going to kill me, I'd die.

183

Colm	It's all right, Aisling, Helen; it turned out to be benign.
Aisling	Oh, thank God.
Colm	But as soon as I got the all-clear, I made a decision there and then that I was out of the rat race and they could stuff their classrooms and staff rooms and life insurance and promotions because I was free, alive, and from now on, my life would be gloriously unpredictable, exciting, dangerous and irresponsible. From now, I'd spend my time finding answers to questions I'd never asked myself, discovering terrains I never thought existed, and the last thing I would ever worry about would be the future – like Jean-Paul Sartre, I was suddenly 'condemned to be free'.
Helen	Oh, I love Jean-Paul Sartre.
Colm	So I asked for a year, but hopefully it'll be a lifetime, a new and better lifetime, starting all over again.
Aisling	I wish I could do that – start all over again.
Helen	Oh, it would be so wonderful.
Colm	Believe me, it *is* wonderful – and tonight is the beginning. That's why I'm here – for the haunting, then Sunday it's the harbour swim, maybe the 10K race tomorrow, and do you know what I'm really looking forward to in the morning? The bungee jump. I just love the bungee jump.
Aisling	Oh, so do . . . *(sees Helen's reaction)* . . . lots of other people.

Colm	From now on, everything is a challenge and I'll also be finding time to discover myself – socially *(Helen and Aisling sigh)*, intellectually *(another sigh)*, even sexually *(a more sensual sigh)* – so, at the end of my life, I'll be able to look back on something actually achieved. And here's to that. *(Drinks)*
Helen	Absolutely, Colm.
Aisling	*(Merrily)* Yes, hear, hear.
Larry	*(Coldly)* So from now on, you've no job?
Colm	No – but I have some cash put by . . .
Larry	. . . oh yes, from living with your aunt . . .
Colm	Exactly – and with my qualifications, I might do some private tuition, or perhaps subbing, anywhere in Europe that I find myself. In short, do whatever I want.
Larry	*(Controlled)* I see. And you're also doing the bungee jump tomorrow?
Colm	*(Excited)* I'm doing the lot. If they had an event where I had to swim stark naked across the lake, climb out, dripping wet, and then run across the fields in my pelt, whipping myself with nettles, I'd do that too.
Helen	I don't think they have that.
Aisling	*(To Helen, quietly)* Unfortunately.
Larry	*(Coldly)* The problem, of course, with your bungee jump, Colm, is that it may have to be cancelled due to the thunderstorm forecast for tomorrow.
Colm	*(Merrily)* Ah – except that the forecast I heard said fine weather tomorrow and the thunderstorm tonight.

185

Larry	Not the one I heard – the one I heard said fine weather tonight and the thunderstorm tomorrow.
Colm	Not the one I heard, Larry.
Larry	*(Sharper)* Well, it was on the one I heard, Colm.
Helen	And where did you hear the one you heard, Larry?
Larry	Where do you think, Helen? Do you think I heard it from a few fellows down in the pub? Or maybe Jean-Paul Sartre told me!
Helen	I'm just asking, did you hear it on the radio or did you actually phone in . . . ?
Larry	*(Angrily)* Yes, Helen, I heard it on the radio and I actually phoned in and I read it in all the newspapers and I watched it on all the television stations including RTÉ, ITV, BBC, TV3 and even T-na-bloody-G-4, or whatever they call it now.
Aisling	And could you actually understand it on TG4?
Larry	*(Furious)* Yes, I could, Aisling – I understood it in every language you can think of and they all said the same thing: fine weather tonight and thunderstorms tomorrow – so, sorry, Colm, believe what you like, but you can take it from me you'll be having no bungee jump tomorrow, much as you'd like to.
Colm	Well, we'll see.
Larry	*(Hard)* Yes, we will see, we will bloody well see . . . *(Turns furiously to Aisling)* . . . and how many more times are you going to point that teapot at me, or are you doing this deliberately or what?

Larry furiously turns the teapot and sweeps the cutlery, plates and cups off the table and sends them crashing across the room. Silence. Then Helen moves to pick them up.

Larry   *(Shouts)* Leave them, Helen, for Christ's sake, leave them!

Helen   Larry . . .

Larry   *(Louder)* And for once in our lives, can we have a bit of disorder around us, or as soon as anyone stops eating, does everything always have to be snapped up, washed, dried, polished and put away in exactly the same bloody way every time? Does it? Well, does it!

Silence. Helen sits. Then:

Colm   *(Quietly)* Larry, sorry about all that . . . but I'd just like to say that it's now coming up to eleven o'clock, and . . .

Larry   *(Quietly)* What? Oh, absolutely right. And thank you very much for that, Colm. *(Trying)* I think we may have taken our eye off the ball there with our little debate – and it's always good to debate, I enjoy debate, always have, the whole cut and thrust of differing opinions – but, good point, time now I think for us to move towards that magical moment. I'll set up my tape recorder – get some new batteries into it, taking no chances tonight – and, if you've time, Colm, I'd really like you to read up on some detail in the book before . . .

Colm   Absolutely – I'll do that right away. *(Gets the book)*

Larry sets up his tape recorder, as:

Helen	*(Annoyed)* And I'll now clear away these things . . .
Larry	*(Lightly)* It's all right, Helen, leave them.

Aisling has left the teapot pointing to where Larry has now moved.

Helen	*(Urgent whisper)* Aisling! The teapot!
Aisling	Oh, sorry. *(Quickly moves it)*
Larry	You all right, Aisling?
Aisling	*(Fearfully)* Yes, thank you.
Larry	Good girl. And sorry about the teapot thing – I just don't like things pointing at me. Something from my childhood, I expect – who knows.
Helen	Larry, I'd really like to clear these things away . . .
Larry	*(To Aisling)* The same way that Helen can't have a dirty cup or a soiled table within a mile of her – everything always has to be perfect, nothing out of place. *(To Helen)* I knew you wouldn't leave that picture hanging crooked for long.
Helen	*(Nervously)* The picture? But I didn't . . .
Larry	*(To Aisling)* And once someone is like that, you can't really blame them. Am I right, Helen?
Helen	*(Annoyed)* I don't know – but I'd really like to clean all this up.
Aisling	If you like, I can put them down in the kitchen for you.
Larry	Well, all right then, one of you, but you'd better go now – I'd like us all seated in here, all in place, at ten past at the latest.

Helen, Aisling and Colm quickly gather the cutlery, etc.

Colm	Helen, I'll do that with Aisling . . .
Helen	No, Colm, I'd like to . . .
Colm	No, you got it ready.
Helen	Please . . . *(Tries to clear the table)*
Colm	*(Firmly)* You stay there. We're doing it. *(She sits)*
Larry	Colm, aren't you supposed to be reading that book for me?
Colm	Don't worry, I can speed-read it when I get back.
Larry	*(Coldly)* Speed-read it? I see. Great.
Colm	We'll just put them in the sink below – no washing up or anything.
Aisling	OK. Just down and back.
Larry	*(Merrily)* And if you meet Annie Ross, tell her she only has twenty minutes.
Colm	*(Merrily)* I might leave her my wristwatch.

Aisling and Colm go. Larry puts the batteries into his tape recorder.

Larry	*(Calls)* Good idea. *(Angrily)* Yes, and leave her some of your schemes as well – Mr Funny man, bloody dosser, bloody turncoat.
Helen	Sorry, Larry?
Larry	No, Helen, I'm sorry, sorry I ever got into this escapade – and far from impressing everyone and getting us to Bromley, this is going to bloody destroy us – you mark my words.
Helen	No, Larry . . .

189

Larry	No? With that fellow now competing against us with his bungee-jumping . . .
Helen	But if the weather . . .
Larry	And all your ooohing and aaaawing at him, as if he was somebody wonderful . . .
Helen	I wasn't . . .
Larry	When all he is is a waster, a drop-out, a born-again dosser, no better than the gutties that broke into the building society – or maybe you'd be ooohing at them too if you met them.
Helen	Larry, that's not fair . . .
Larry	And he bloody well despises me.
Helen	He doesn't . . .
Larry	Of course he does. He's out in the world – free, independent, living dangerously – while I'm still in the rat race, locked into my little hole of an office, eating cheese sandwiches with all the other rats.
Helen	*(Angrily)* He was only being conversational – and Larry, I didn't straighten that picture.
Larry	Everyone against me – you, him, her, everyone. Well, I'll show you all – I'll make this night work if it bloody well kills me.

Colm comes in.

Helen	Ah, Colm . . .
Larry	Colm. Everything in order?
Colm	Perfect. Aisling insisted on washing.
Helen	Oh dear, I could have done that.
Larry	And did you 'speed-read' the book yet?

Colm	I'll do that now.
Larry	*(Controlled)* Because we only have fifteen minutes to go, and I'd like you to be able to give us a picture of what exactly to expect here – and maybe you'd tell me if they say she comes in that door or that door?
Colm	I'll skip to that.
Helen	Larry, do you know where the loo is?
Larry	Helen, you're not serious – we have less than fifteen minutes.
Helen	Three minutes, Larry.
Colm	Second door on the landing, Helen.
Helen	Thank you, Colm.
Colm	There's a light in the loo but none on the landing, so take a torch.
Helen	Right. *(Goes to stage-left door. Opens it. Looks into the blackness. Nervously)* And leave this door open.
Larry	And don't be all night, Helen.

Aisling comes in the stage-right door from the kitchen.

Helen	Ah, Aisling, I'm going out to the loo.
Larry	For God's sake, Helen – why don't you open the window and tell the whole countryside?
Helen	I'm only asking if she wants to come.
Aisling	No, I'm fine. Thanks.
Helen	OK. *(Nervously)* I suppose I'll go on my own so.

Helen goes, with the torch, leaving the door open.

Aisling	Ten minutes to go.

191

Larry	Give or take.
Aisling	I think I'll hold her photo in my hand. For when she comes. *(Removes a photo from the album)*
Larry	And that's an excellent idea, Aisling, and you can give it plenty of atmosphere, say exactly what you're doing and what you expect to see. *(Into his microphone)* One, two, three, testing, one, two, three.
Colm	This is a bit hard to believe.
Aisling	What is?
Colm	*(The book)* Michael Hamilton's version of events.
Larry.	Does he say she comes that way or this way?
Colm	Oh, that door *(Stage right)* from the kitchen.
Larry	Thank you. *(Sets his microphone)*
Colm	But he doesn't really explain why Annie Ross knifed Stephen, paralysed him for life and then killed herself – hardly because he wouldn't marry her.
Larry	No, because she was raving mad – the Hamiltons never made any secret of that.
Colm	But Stephen did once want to marry her.
Aisling	Does it say anything about a baby?

Helen runs in the stage-left door, breathless.

Larry	Are you all right, Helen?
Helen	*(Nervously. Closes the door)* Yes. I didn't think it would be so dark out there and cobwebs every-where – but the toilet is lovely, isn't it, Colm – the old chain and everything?
Colm	Yes, and that lovely ornamental bowl.

192

Helen	The Victorians loved those – I did an evening class once about . . .
Larry	Helen, could we have your observations on lavatories some other time – Colm is now going to give us the official Michael Hamilton version of the haunting so we'll know how to react.
Helen	*(Nervously)* God, I hate this – I hope I won't have to go again.
Larry	Then for God's sake go now, Helen!
Helen	*(Angrily)* How can I go now, I've just come back . . . it's all right, I'm fine, I'm fine. Sorry, Colm.
Colm	No problem, Helen. So, basically, Michael Hamilton says that in the years they lived here, from 1932 to 1939, on most anniversaries after her death, they used to sit in this room waiting, and then they would usually become aware of a coldness in the air and shortly after that would begin to hear her below, around the kitchen area, and then they'd hear her footsteps on the wooden stairs, coming up, coming closer and closer, and they always knew exactly when she was outside that door . . .
Aisling	It was really very cold down in the kitchen just now.
Helen	Oh, Christ.
Larry	Go on, Colm.
Colm	And she would seem to stay outside the door for a while and then there'd be a very definite sensation that her presence had entered the room and she seemed to linger over there for

some moments and then they knew she was moving across, towards them –

Helen   *(Nervously)* Colm, please . . .

Colm   No, this is good, Helen, listen: *(Reads)* ' . . . and we would remain sitting, Stephen in his wheel-chair with father and mother close to him and I nearby, and we would wait and then we'd have a greater awareness of the coldness in the room and whenever Annie Ross seemed at peace – when she wasn't angry and moving furniture or rattling doors – there would be just the sensation of someone moving slowly across the room, silently except for the rustle of her clothes, passing close to each of us, as though observing us, and, on two occasions, she stopped at Stephen's wheelchair and suddenly we saw it move a little and father immediately clipped on the wheel-brakes and it tugged angrily against them and Stephen was breathing more heavily, but then it stopped and she moved on and then we knew that she had reached the opposite door' – that one – 'and, at this moment, always, we would begin to hear the sobbing and when that happened, Stephen would almost growl in anger and mother would clasp his paralysed hand and, in Stephen's eyes, would be the look of absolute hatred while the sobbing continued at the door and then we'd hear the rustling of clothes and then, at last, her footsteps beyond the door, on the landing, moving away, and we would wait in total silence, looking at each

194

other, until Stephen would nod and we would know that her evil spirit was gone from us, for another year.'

Silence

Larry	And that, everybody, gives us the perfect setting of what we should expect and what we should react to and also perfect timing – we have three minutes to go.
Aisling	We should be hearing her in the kitchen soon.
Colm	Get all my protection in place. *(Holds his garlic, cross and knife)*
Helen	*(Nervously. Quietly)* Jesus, is any promotion worth this?
Larry	Just relax, Helen.
Helen	*(Nervously)* I'll be glad when it's all over.
Colm	Larry, OK if I'm in the wheelchair?
Larry	*(Disappointed)* What? *(Then)* All right. Sure. OK.
Colm	Brakes on, just in case.
Aisling	*(Waiting with the photo)* Nothing yet.
Larry	Two minutes everybody, so pay attention now. Remember, we're the first people to be in here on this night since the Hamiltons had to leave . . .
Colm	Except for Jason Sweeney . . .
Larry	Oh, right . . .
Aisling	And I think he saw her that night and that's what killed him.
Larry	And it's no bad thing, Aisling, if you say that, because in exactly one minute, I'll be pressing the record button and then, folks, everything we say

on this recording will be played on the Gerry Ryan show in the morning, so we all need to give it two or three minutes of good, spooky atmosphere, as if Annie Ross was right here among us.

Immediately a flash of lightning and a crack of thunder. The room lights flicker.

Helen   My God, what's that?

Colm   *(Excitedly)* Lightning – and thunder.

Helen   Oh Jesus. *(Blesses herself)*

Colm   You know what this means?

Aisling   *(Watching)* Yes, that she is coming . . . that she's definitely coming now.

Larry   It means that now we'll have a great, natural atmosphere for the recording.

Colm   No, Larry – it means that my forecast was right – and it'll be fine for my bungee jump tomorrow.

Larry   *(Annoyed)* For Christ's sake, can we all just concentrate on one thing at a time. Remember that this is not the shagging bungee jump, this is the haunting, nothing else. *(Then)* OK, eleven-nineteen, this is it, folks, here we go.

Larry presses the record button. All face the closed stage-right door. Silence. Then:

Aisling   *(Quietly)* Annie? Annie Ross? Is that you, Annie? Are you coming up the stairs, Annie, are you coming to us? Is that you, Annie? Is it?

Helen   *(Nervously)* Oh my God, help us.

A flicker of lightning, a rumble of thunder, as they watch, as we fade to blackout.

End of Act One

ACT TWO

Scene One

Same set. Same time. We open with a slight overlap of dialogue to re-establish.

Aisling   *(Quietly)* Annie? Annie Ross? Is that you, Annie? Are you coming up the stairs, Annie, are you coming to us? Is that you, Annie? Is it?

Helen   *(Nervously)* Oh my God, help us.

Another minor flash of lightning – the lights flicker, there's a low rumble of thunder.

Aisling   *(Quietly)* Annie? Annie? Annie? Annie?

Helen   *(Nervously)* Maybe it'd be better not to keep calling her.

Larry   *(Quietly)* No, that's good. *(Then)* Wait a minute, I think I can feel something.

Helen   What? What do you feel?

Larry   Not quite sure . . . but there's definitely something.

Colm moves in the wheelchair.

198

Larry	*(Hopefully)* Did that move? Did your wheelchair move, Colm – *(into the microphone)* the one that Stephen Hamilton used to sit in?
Colm	I don't think so.
Larry	*(Prompting)* I thought I saw it moving.
Colm	No, I did that. *(Moves it again)* Frankly, I don't think there's anything happening at all.
Helen	*(Hopefully)* No, and neither do I.
Larry	*(Loudly)* No, no, there *is* something – I'm very aware of something very definite in here now.
Helen	Well, I'm not, Larry.
Colm	Me neither.
Larry	*(Hand over the microphone. Furious)* For God's sake, what are you trying to do? This is for the radio.
Colm	*(Realising)* Oh, right. Sorry. *(Loudly)* Yes, there is something now.
Larry	*(Prompting)* Helen!
Helen	*(Trying)* Oh yes, there is a . . . coldness in the air.
Larry	Yes, and a rustling of clothes – seems to be passing through. *(Prompting)* Colm!
Colm	*(Loudly)* Yes. Wait a minute, I think the wheelchair moved. Yes, there is definitely something moving it now.
Helen	*(Flatly)* It's very spooky.
Larry	*(Annoyed, but overriding Helen's contribution)* Oh yes, there is undoubtedly something in here with us now. This is very frightening – no doubt, this is a haunted room all right.

A rumble of thunder. Larry holds up the microphone to catch it.

Colm	And doesn't it remind us of those great Louis MacNeice lines? *(Colm seems to forget them, to Larry's consternation. Then . . .)* 'A house can be haunted by those who were never there/if there was where they were missed.'
Larry	*(Lost)* You took the words out of my mouth, Colm. What's that?

A rumble of thunder

Colm	More thunder.
Larry	Oh, I can feel my heart thumping . . . *(Helen imitates the heartbeat sound with her hand on her chest. Larry angrily signals her to stop. Then . . .)* This really is a haunting. And this is Larry Synott, in the presence of the ghost of Annie Ross, in the haunted house where once she lived and now lives on in spirit, saying goodbye, knowing that a long and frightening night awaits us in this cold, quiet, supernatural place.

Larry presses the button, turning off the machine.

Larry	*(Delighted)* Great! That was terrific – well done, everybody.
Helen	*(Relieved and happy)* I was beginning to frighten myself there.
Colm	And the thunder was right on cue.
Larry	It was all first-class, couldn't have been better – and your poem, Colm – brilliant.
Helen	I love MacNeice – what was that from?

200

Larry	*(Merrily)* It's all right, Helen, this isn't your literature-appreciation class – the important thing is that it sounded spot on.
Colm	*(Merrily)* Hey, supposing Annie Ross *had* arrived?
Helen	Oh, stop it, Colm.
Larry	*(Merrily)* We'd've got her to join in – give us a wail or something. *(Wails)*
Helen	Well, I'm only glad it's all over. Though, frankly, I still don't fancy going down to the kitchen to fill my hot-water bottles.
Larry	No need to do that yet, Helen.
Colm	I want to finish this book before turning in.
Larry	Well, I think that now that our mission is complete and we have our tape, it's time to relax.
Helen	Still, I'd like my sleeping bag nice and warm . . .
Larry	Helen likes her comforts – off you go, then.
Helen	Won't be long – Aisling, would you like to . . . ? *('come with me' is implied)*

They now realise that Aisling is sobbing, having put the photo aside.

Helen	*(Goes to her)* Oh, Aisling. Oh I'm so sorry – you really wanted her to come, didn't you?
Aisling	*(Sobbing)* Doesn't matter.
Helen	Oh dear. *(To Colm)* Her mother.
Colm	OK. *(Goes to Aisling. Caring)* OK, Aisling, you listen carefully now: maybe we didn't notice anything, maybe she didn't come . . .
Larry	*(Anxiously)* Though we're not saying that . . .
Colm	*(To Aisling)* . . . but that doesn't mean that

201

nothing happened. Like, did you feel anything
at all?

Aisling   *(Angrily)* No, I didn't, because there's nothing to
feel and nothing to see . . .

Helen   Oh, now . . .

Aisling   . . . because there *is* nothing!

Colm   No, Aisling, none of this means there is nothing . . .

Aisling   Well, she didn't come, did she?

Larry   No, no, I felt something.

Aisling   No, you didn't; no one felt anything.

Helen   I felt frightened.

Aisling   It's all pretend, all a cover-up, nothing happened
and we all know it.

Larry   *(Anxiously)* For God's sake, Aisling, you can't be
saying that.

Colm   No, Aisling, listen, I know what you're thinking,
but just because nothing happened *here* . . .

Larry   *(Anxiously)* And I wish you'd all stop saying
that – we have to convince people out there that
something . . .

Colm   *(Angrily)* We know that – this is only between
ourselves! This is not for outside.

Larry   Right – because we have to think of the pledges,
we have to think of the starving children.

Colm   Aisling, maybe Annie Ross didn't come . . .

Aisling   I should have faced up to it from the beginning . . .

Helen   . . . no, Aisling . . .

Aisling   . . . mammy is dead and that's it and I'll never see
her again, never know what she thought or . . .

202

Helen	No, she's out there and she understands . . .
Aisling	She's not – she's gone and everything else is all lies put into our heads to make us feel better, but nobody comes back and I didn't see her at the end of my bed . . .
Helen	No, no, you did . . .
Aisling	*(Angrily)* I didn't! I only thought I did because I wanted to think it, the same as we all go around telling each other bare-faced lies to stop us thinking about the truth – and I'm sick and tired of it, of all this messing and all this make-believe and all this carry-on too and you might as well know that I don't give a shite about you or your starving children or your promotion or your radio programme or Gerry shaggin' Ryan because this is just a waste of time and I'm sick of it and I'm out of here . . . *(Packing her things)* . . . I'm out of here this instant and don't anyone try to stop me.
Larry	*(Panic)* No, no, you can't do that.
Aisling	You watch me. *(Packing)*
Helen	No, Aisling . . .
Larry	But the door is locked and the alarms are set . . .
Aisling	Then I'll break the shagging door and set off the alarms, because I'm out of here and I'm out of here now.
Larry	*(For help)* Colm, she can't go!
Colm	No, Aisling, no – please, listen to me for just a minute. Just a minute. OK? Please? Just sit here a moment. Please?

She stops, still sobbing.

Colm	OK. Because I, Aisling, of all people, know exactly how you feel. *(To all)* And maybe, everybody, maybe it is best if we are absolutely honest about everything from now on – best if here, between ourselves, we tell it exactly as we believe it, in our hearts.
Larry	Absolutely.
Helen	Of course.
Larry	*(Quietly and anxiously)* Just as long as she stays.
Colm	Because Aisling, the truth, regarding where your mother is or where Annie Ross is or Jason Sweeney or what happens to anyone who dies, is that nobody really has the slightest idea. We have no idea, none of us, as to what is there for any of us beyond the moment of death.
Larry	*(Lost)* Absolutely.
Colm	We are all flying blind – and, OK, some of us fall back on faith, some rely on fantasy, some of us speculate, some of us just fool ourselves, but, at the end of the day, not even the greatest minds of their time had the answer – Voltaire, Einstein, Kierkegaard, Isaac Newton . . .
Larry	. . . Eamon Dunphy. The list is endless.
Colm	*(Patiently)* Right. None of them knew for certain what was going to happen, or if *anything* was going to happen – *I* didn't know when I found myself at death's door . . .
Larry	He was there, Aisling.
Colm	And in years to come, after all my searching into

	myself for answers and reasons, I know that I still won't know – but I will know more about not knowing, and at least I will have made the search, and that's the best any of us can do.
Helen	Exactly – all we can do is make the search.
Colm	Exactly.
Larry	*(Lost)* Exactly.
Colm	And OK, Annie Ross doesn't seem to have come this year, but maybe, just maybe, she was here last year and maybe will be here next year and, if so, will we ever know why she misses a year?
Larry	Exactly – like the plums on my plum tree.
Colm	Pardon, Larry?
Larry	Like the plum tree we have in the back garden – haven't we, Helen?
Helen	What about it, darling?
Larry	Full of plums this year; next year, nothing. The following year plenty of plums, but now they've all been eaten by wasps, next year not a wasp to be seen and we have a bumper harvest of plums and, no matter how you look at it, there's no explanation.
Colm	*(Patiently)* Right. And the world is full of similar questions and very few answers, and we never achieve anything by running away, but we owe it to our very existence to stay and join in the search.
Helen	*(Kindly)* Do you understand what Colm is saying, Aisling, about his search?
Larry	Or what I'm saying.
Helen	Or what Larry is saying about . . . about his plums?

205

Aisling	*(Sadly)* I don't think I understand anything any more.
Colm	And that, Aisling, is the best answer you could possibly give. As Eliot put it: 'Where is the wisdom we have lost in knowledge/ Where is the knowledge lost in information.'
Larry	Exactly. *(Concerned)* And you're not going home now, are you?
Aisling	*(Quietly)* No.
Larry	Good. That's great. *(Quietly to Helen)* We're OK.
Colm	And remember, Aisling, not knowing about death is not so extraordinary – it is only one of a million things we don't know, but blindly accept.
Larry	Absolutely.
Colm	And as we have a minute, let me say this – that since my brush with death, *I've* been acutely aware about what I *don't* know – about me, who I am, or what I am, or if I am only what I appear to be and, always, there is the growing realisation that it is only a random gamble of nature that we are here at all, in this place, it is only a throw of the dice that we weren't all born in a slum in Hong Kong and what would we be then, what would we be doing all day?
Larry	Probably pulling rickshaws, with the arses out of our trousers.
Colm	And not only that, but here, now, as we are, how can we be sure that we are what we seem to be, or are we merely what society demands us to be. Take any of us – take me, take Larry: here we

206

are, dressed like men, behaving like men, shaving every morning like men – but how do we know we *are* men? Supposing we had time to search, to explore other options regarding gender, attractions, impulses, real selves? But we don't, so we accept life, roles, without question. Am I right, Larry?

Larry *(Lost)* Oh, absolutely.

Colm Like, how do I not know that I am not naturally a gifted fashion designer or Larry is not a skilled architect? Or, for argument's sake, let's take the most fantastic and say how do I know that, despite appearances, that I am really a man, or that Larry is not really a woman?

Larry *(In shock. Then . . .)* Well, Colm, in fairness, I do have a few bits and pieces that suggest . . .

Colm No, no, not physically – I mean in here *(His head)*, where you are privately most comfortable...or uncomfortable. Do you know what I mean, Larry?

Larry To be perfectly honest . . .

Colm Like, we never take time to explore that question, do we? But the fact is that, inside each of us, you and me, Larry, who's to say that there's not a woman trying desperately to get out?

Larry *(Reaches for the whiskey)* Well, if there is, I haven't noticed her.

Colm That's what I'm saying – it's another unexplored question.

Larry Well, it might be for you, Colm . . .

Colm No, it is for all of us.

Helen That's very true, Larry.

207

Larry	What's very true, Helen?
Helen	I mean, how does any of us know for sure . . .
Larry	*(Annoyed)* What exactly are you saying, Helen?
Colm	*(Lightly)* Well, to follow through the point, what I'm certainly *not* saying is that, to find out, we should suddenly start wearing tights and putting on bras . . .
Larry	*(Annoyed)* Well, that's a relief. *(Drinks)*
Colm	But you should think of what it means, if only to eliminate it.
Larry	Listen, would you mind addressing these suggestions to yourself, and not to me?
Colm	But I am.
Larry	Good – so what you are saying is *you'd* like to dress up in . . .
Colm	No, I'm saying I *could*, we all could . . .
Larry	No, you're saying *you* could . . .
Colm	OK, I'm saying *I* could . . .
Larry	But not me.
Colm	But how do you know?
Larry	*(Angrily)* How do I know? I'll tell you how I know – I know because I bloody well know, that's how I know.
Colm	But if you've never even thought about it . . .
Larry	And I have no intention of thinking about it, never mind doing it.
Helen	*(Lightly)* Although you once did, darling.
Larry	I once did what?
Helen	Remember that fancy-dress we went to years ago and you . . .
Larry	Helen, we are not talking about how we dress

	at fancy-dresses, we are talking about how we dress in life.
Colm	Except that how we *choose* to dress at fancy-dresses may indicate how we *desire* to dress in life.
Larry	Except I didn't choose.
Helen	Oh, Larry, yes you did.
Larry	Helen, I did not. From the very start, I always wanted to go as a gorilla.
Helen	No, Larry.
Larry	Yes, Helen, it was you . . .
Helen	No, Larry, it was you, you even hired the wig and bought the balloons . . .
Larry	I did not
Helen	. . . and said it would be great if you went as Dolly Parton.
Larry	That was all your idea, Helen – and anyway, I don't know why we're talking about that here, I thought we were here to talk about dead people coming back from the dead.
Colm	Of course – and we also owe it to ourselves to explore everything in equal measure, to ask the dangerous questions . . .
Helen	That's very true.
Larry	That's the second time you've said that, Helen.
Colm	And that's probably because, as a woman, Helen knows more than we do.
Larry	Knows more about what?
Colm	More about what her inner self is saying, how it speaks to her and, crucially, how she responds to these subconscious impulses.
Larry	Oh, that's it! I've had enough of this crap. I'm

	out of this game. *(Moves and drinks)*
Helen	Larry, don't . . .
Larry	No choice, Helen – no man could stay sober and listen to that shit.
Helen	Larry!
Larry	*(To Helen)* And incidentally, have you forgotten what I said to you earlier when you were going on about me having a glass eye?
Helen	Oh Larry, everyone knows you haven't got a glass eye!
Larry	Yes, and now when I'm being interviewed for this job, after I've convinced them that I haven't got a glass eye, will I now have to explain that no, I don't feel more comfortable in a pair of knickers, and if, by some shagging accident, they *do* give me the job, that I won't want to sit behind my desk in Bromley dressed up as Dolly Parton.
Helen	Larry, no one's going to know . . .
Larry	And you're dead right, no one's going to know, because I want no more of this crap-talk *(To Colm)* and you may think that this is all very academic and interesting and worthy of idle debate – but I'm getting just a bit sick of being goaded into answering your questions . . .
Colm	I'm not goading you . . .
Larry	If you want to go off and find answers, off you go . . .
Helen	Larry!
Larry	*(Aggressively)* But the only answer I want, right now, is if all these twisted ideas of yours are

210

	something new, or if you had them when you were down at the school teaching our two sons!
Helen	Oh, for God's sake, Larry . . .
Larry	And Helen, you should want an answer to that question too – or would you prefer to wait until, some weekend, our boys come over to visit us, dressed as the two Ugly Sisters?
Helen	*(Quietly)* Larry, the doctor clearly told you that while you're on that medication, you should never . . . *('take alcohol' is implied)*
Larry	*(More controlled)* And that, Colm, is my question: did you or did you not have all these peculiar ideas while you were teaching and influencing . . . ?
Colm	*(Loud and angry)* And the answer is no! This is a debate, this is a questioning of life – and it was born of me having my scare, not before!
Larry	*(Angrily)* Or so you'd like us to believe!
Helen	*(Angrily)* Larry, you have no right . . .
Larry	Oh, have I not? Well, let me tell you, if he continues this shit for much longer and only *half* of it gets out, you can forget Bromley and your new house and your new evening classes and your new tennis club and the new Bobby Andrews, whoever he may bloody well turn out to be.
Helen	*(Angrily)* What's Bobby Andrews got to do with anything?
Larry	*(Hard)* Well, you tell me, Helen – you tell me.

Silence. A distant rumble of thunder.

Colm	So, Aisling, what I'm saying – and leaving aside all questions of identity and choice and gender . . .
Larry	Good!
Colm	. . . is that we can never be sure of anything, either of ourselves or of outside forces, so whether Annie Ross comes here or not, whether your mother appeared to you or not, there is still as much chance of her being in an afterlife as there is not. But if she *is* there, there is every chance that she sees you, understands you, forgives you, loves you – and that is the best we can ever hope for.
Aisling	Except that I can't. There's other things.
Colm	Other things?
Aisling	About me and Keith.
Colm	Keith? Your boyfriend?
Aisling	Ex. *(Then)* And the real reason we broke up was because, two months after that night, I discovered I was pregnant.
Larry	*(Quietly)* Good God – what next!
Aisling	And I know it's stupid and everything . . .
Colm	No, no . . .
Aisling	But the way it happened that night, the timing and everything, I worked it out that mammy died at about the exact time as me and Keith were . . . that the baby was being conceived.
Helen	Oh dear.
Aisling	And the way I was thinking, I then thought, from that moment, that my baby wouldn't just be my baby, that she'd really be . . . mammy, coming back again.
Larry	Jesus, I don't believe this.

212

Colm	Ah, as in reincarnation – as the spirit departs, the spirit appears.
Larry	He's off again – another debate!
Aisling	Exactly, reincarnation – and then I was really happy, really looking forward to the baby being born, to seeing mammy again.
Larry	*(Quietly)* Still whistling, I suppose.
Aisling	But when I told Keith, he went ballistic – said I should see a psychiatrist and that the pregnancy was all my fault and nothing to do with him and it was all over between us and he never wanted to see me again.
Helen	Oh dear.
Aisling	And up to then I was really looking forward to it, to mammy, and I had even bought this lovely pink cradle, with little toys hanging all around it and little bells and everything. *(Pause)* But then, after four months, I was so depressed about Keith and everything, I went over to a friend of mine in London and, with the worry and everything, I lost my baby.
Helen	London? Oh Aisling, you didn't . . . ? *('have an abortion' is implied)*
Aisling	No, no – it wasn't like Annie Ross or anything, I didn't do what she did or anything . . .
Colm	What she did? What did she do?
Aisling	Like Mrs Campion said, how she got pregnant and Stephen was raging and said he'd only marry her if she didn't have the baby and the Hamilton family paid for her to go to London . . .
Colm	*(Of the Hamilton book)* Yes, it makes sense . . .

213

Aisling	. . . and Mrs Campion says she got rid of it and came back but then he'd changed his mind and that's why she knifed him – but I wasn't like that, I never did that, that's not why I went to London . . .
Colm	No, of course not.
Aisling	I think I lost it because I was so upset about Keith and everything – and that's what happened. Not like Annie Ross . . .
Helen	No . . .
Aisling	But the thing is, that after London and all, mammy never appeared to me again. *(Sadly)* But now I know that her appearing was probably all my imagination anyway and that when people die, it *is* the end and they're gone and they don't come back . . . and I don't care what anyone says about anything any more.

Pause

Larry	Just one thing, Aisling . . .
Helen	Please, Larry . . .
Larry	That story about Annie Ross in London . . .
Aisling	That's not a story, it's what old Mrs . . .
Larry	And it's a bloody lie, because the Hamiltons are a respectable family and long-time clients of ours and we've acted for them for years and I don't want that slander mentioned again to anyone anywhere any more.
Aisling	*(Angrily)* And who would I mention it to, for Christ's sake?

214

Larry	*(Angrily)* Just don't mention it to anyone!
Aisling	*(Angrily)* I won't − and I don't want anything about me mentioned to anyone either.
Larry	And it won't be.
Aisling	*(Shouts)* It better not be.

Silence

Larry	*(Brighter)* Right. Good. And now, after all that, after our little exchange of ideas, of opinions − and nothing wrong with that, I enjoy debate, always have − but now we should really think of turning in, get our sleeping bags set up, because, media-wise, I think we will have exciting times ahead of us from tomorrow.
Colm	I may read some more of this book . . .
Larry	Oh yes, do − and any details you come across that may be of use to me on the radio.

Larry turns on his radio. Gentle music.

Larry	Ah, I love that. Bit of easy listening to prepare us for sleep. And Helen, you wanted to fill your hot-water bottles?
Helen	*(Still annoyed)* Oh, yes . . .
Larry	Here, I'll do that for you.
Helen	No, no, I don't mind now.
Larry	No, give them here to me, I'll look after them for you. *(Quietly to Helen)* And from now on, let's just keep everything nice and simple.
Helen	*(Quietly)* It wasn't me who . . .

215

Larry	(*Quietly*) And the less said to that one the better – Keith was right, she is a head case.
Helen	All she needs is . . .
Larry	And don't put our sleeping bags anywhere near that other weirdo tonight . . .
Helen	Oh, Larry . . .
Larry	. . . and I'm keeping the light on – because I personally wouldn't be too surprised to see him climbing into a little pink nightdress . . .
Helen	Larry, that's not fair – he was merely debating . . .
Larry	And can we now forget the debates and have a good night's sleep because we have a great tape with great stories and if we just survive the next few hours, we're home and dry. (*Brightly*) You all right, Aisling? Can I get you a drink of water or anything?
Aisling	I might get one later, thanks.
Larry	Excellent – and a good night's sleep will do you the world of good. Colm, you OK there?
Colm	Fine. (*Of the book*) This is very good.
Larry	Excellent – and I've no problem with you keeping the light on if you want to read late.
Colm	Oh, thanks.
Larry	No problem. Back in a jiffy.
Helen	(*Calls*) And make sure the water is boiling, Larry.
Larry	(*Calls*) Don't worry.

Larry is gone with the two hot-water bottles. The music plays gently. Colm reads.

Helen	About Annie Ross, Aisling – if you don't mind –

	but did she really go to London to . . . ?
Aisling	That's what Mrs Campion said – that she had a sister in London, also in service, and she stayed with her until she was better again and she was sure when she came back that Stephen would marry her . . .
Helen	The poor thing.
Aisling	But, Mrs Campion says, she then found out he was already engaged to another girl – Amanda something-or-other whose family owned horses and everything.
Colm	*(Of the book)* Hey, look at this – we may have to get Larry back for this.
Helen	For what, Colm?
Colm	Much more detailed stuff on the hauntings in this chapter, and, it says, in the eight years that the Hamiltons were here, Annie Ross never came at twenty past eleven.
Helen	What?
Colm	Hamilton says here: 'Always, her presence seemed to enter the room on the stroke of midnight.'
Helen	Midnight? But everyone says twenty past eleven . . .
Aisling	It was twenty past eleven that Jason Sweeney . . .
Helen	That's when he died . . .
Colm	Exactly, and I think that's where that time came from – I think he was really waiting for midnight.
Helen	What?
Colm	It says here that because the stabbing was at midnight and Annie Ross left the house at midnight, the hauntings of this room were always at midnight.

217

Aisling	And that's what Mrs Campion said, and I said she was wrong . . .
Helen	And what time is it now?
Aisling	Just gone ten to midnight.
Colm	Listen. *(Reads)* 'In the minutes before midnight, we'd hear her in the house, usually in the kitchens below us . . . '
Helen	*(Realising)* Larry.
Colm	' . . . and then at the stroke of midnight we would know that she was in the room and we would wonder what her mood would be this year . . . '
Helen	Oh my God.
Colm	I really think Larry should be back for this.
Helen	*(Fearfully)* Be back for what? What is there to be back for?
Colm	*(Unsure)* Well . . . to turn on his tape recorder . . .
Helen	But for what? He has a tape already . . .
Colm	Well, for . . . Gerry Ryan – he might know it's midnight, he might ask him about midnight . . .

The radio suddenly crackles and goes dead.

Helen	Colm . . . ?
Colm	*(Goes to it. Then . . .)* It's gone dead – does Larry have spare batteries?
Helen	Spare batteries? He just put new batteries into it . . .
Colm	New batteries?

A rumble of thunder, as:

Helen	Oh Christ! I'll go and tell him. *(Nervously)* Aisling, are you coming with me?
Aisling	What? No, I'll stay here in case . . .
Helen	Oh for God's sake! Colm?
Colm	What? Yes, yes, all right, I'll go down with you . . .

Suddenly, below in the kitchen, a roar of pain and fear. It is Larry.

Helen	*(Stops)* Oh my God, what's that?
Colm	It's Larry! *(Goes)* Come on, quickly. *(Calls)* Larry?
Helen	*(Follows, calling)* Larry? Colm, not so fast, wait for me. Colm, will you wait?

They are gone through the stage-right door. Aisling picks up the book and sits to read it. There is a flicker of lightning now and a rumble of thunder. Now there is the noise of running feet on the wooden stairs. Aisling reads on and we hear:

Larry	*(Off)* Leave me alone – for Christ's sake, leave me alone.
Helen	*(Off)* Stop running, Larry.
Colm	*(Off. Protesting)* I did nothing – I swear.

Larry runs angrily in. He is in pain and has a tea towel wrapped around his left hand. Colm and Helen follow. Aisling stands, as:

Larry	*(Angrily)* Will you just leave it, leave it!
Helen	You have to keep the air out.
Aisling	What happened to you?
Colm	He scalded himself with boiling water.

Larry	*(Of Colm)* Thanks to his shagging, messing and trick-acting. *(In pain)* Jesus.
Colm	But I did nothing.
Larry	And anyway, Helen, I don't know why the hell you have to bring hot-water bottles everywhere you go.
Helen	I would have filled them . . .
Larry	It's a wonder you don't fill one every time you go to the shaggin' jacks. *(His hand)* Christ, it's full of blisters.
Helen	*(With her first-aid box)* Now, here we are – burn-cream, bandage, lint, tweezers, surgical scissors, bandage clips and Rescue Remedy. Hold still.
Larry	Are you prepared for brain surgery as well?
Colm	The sooner you get the cream on, the better.
Larry	And the sooner you grow up the better.
Colm	But I tell you, I didn't do anything.
Larry	No, apart from pushing in the kitchen door, knocking me sideways when I was holding a saucepan of boiling water . . .
Colm	But I didn't . . .
Helen	*(With the cream)* Hold steady.
Larry	*(In pain)* Oh Christ.
Colm	When I got to the kitchen, you were already on the floor with the water all over the place . . .
Larry	*(Painfully)* Helen, you're lifting the skin . . .
Helen	Hold still. *(With the bandage)*
Aisling	*(To Larry)* And did you shout out when you scalded yourself or before you scalded yourself?
Larry	*(Stops)* Are you trying to be funny? I hardly

220

shouted *before* I scalded myself – I can't see into the shagging future . . .

Aisling No, I mean . . .

Larry Though, coming from you, that question doesn't surprise me.

Aisling *(Annoyed)* I'm only asking because we were all here when you shouted – we all heard you . . . including Colm.

Colm Exactly – I ran down, with Helen after me . . .

Helen That's very true, Larry.

Larry You say 'that's very true' just one more time . . .

Helen But we *were* here when you shouted.

Larry I'm not a gobshite, I know what he did – don't try to cover up for him.

Helen I'm not.

Larry I've been watching the pair of you all night.

Helen All I'm saying is maybe you got confused when you got scalded . . .

Larry I'm not confused, I don't get confused – he's been acting the messer since he got here . . .

Colm All right, all right, don't believe me – but the reason we ran down to you was to say that, according to Hamilton's book, the hauntings took place at midnight, not twenty past eleven.

Larry *(Stops)* What?

Helen And we thought Gerry Ryan might know that and . . .

Larry The haunting was at eleven-twenty and we have it on tape and Gerry said eleven-twenty . . .

Colm Maybe because he hadn't read the book . . .

Aisling But in here *(The book)* it says midnight and old

221

	Mrs Campion said midnight . . .
Larry	Show me that shaggin' book. *(Reads)*
Helen	And Gerry Ryan's researchers might find out . . . it could be on the Internet or something . . .
Colm	And now if you want to record at midnight, your batteries have run out . . .
Larry	But even William said it was eleven-twenty . . .
Colm	Or did he say Jason Sweeney died at eleven-twenty?
Larry	The bastard probably said that deliberately to make me look a gobshite. *(Throws the book aside)* Christ, how much time have we got before midnight? *(Looks to his wristwatch – Helen has bandaged over it)* Jesus – Helen!
Colm	Five minutes – but your batteries have run out
Larry	*(Getting spare batteries)* I know, I heard you – and someone must have been blaring it to run them down . . .
Helen	No, we . . .
Larry	*(As he removes and inserts new batteries. To Helen)* Coming here with your bandages, creams, rubber gloves, washing-up liquid – better if you found out a few facts before walking me into this.
Helen	But it wasn't me who . . .
Larry	Oh yes, blame me, why not? Right, we'll do it all over again – we'll continue on the tape from where we stopped. I'd better check that now.

He rewinds the tape.

222

Colm	I think we're OK – four minutes to go.
Helen	Yes, plenty of time.
Aisling	Except that it says in the book that they used to hear her around the house before . . .
Helen	*(Angrily)* We know all that, Aisling!
Aisling	. . . and it says there was always a coldness and a strange smell before her presence . . .
Helen	*(Louder)* And I'd prefer if you'd now shut up about that kind of thing.
Larry	*(Louder)* And I'd prefer if you'd all shut up so I can check this tape.
Aisling	*(Quietly)* And it's getting very cold now.
Colm	And the heater is still on.
Larry	*(Loudly)* Please!

Larry plays the tape, turns up the volume. They listen in silence to:

Larry	*(On tape)* ' . . . and this is Larry Synott, in the presence of the ghost of Annie Ross, in the haunted house where once she lived and now lives on in spirit, saying goodbye, knowing that a long and frightening night awaits us in this cold, quiet, supernatural place.'
Larry	OK, great, that's it . . .

Larry is about to turn it off, but suddenly, clearly, on the tape, is the distinctive sound of a girl sobbing.

Helen	What's that?
Colm	It's . . . it's someone crying.
Larry	How the hell did that get there?

Aisling	It's not me.
Larry	*(Angrily turns it off)* That's it – it *is* you! You were crying just after that because you wanted to give birth to your shaggin' mother.
Colm	But Larry, we were *all* here talking then.
Helen	That's very true, Larry.
Larry	*(Angrily to Helen)* Once more, Helen!
Helen	But we *were* all talking when Aisling was crying – why are we not on it?
Aisling	And anyway, it's not me.
Colm	Is it an old tape, Larry – is it one you had at home?
Larry	*(Angrily)* You mean do I have all these tapes at home of women crying? What kind of a pervert do you think I am?
Helen	Unless, Aisling, you were crying here when Colm and I ran down . . .
Aisling	No, I was reading here . . .
Colm	*(Nervously)* And Larry, I swear to God, I didn't open that kitchen door down there . . .
Larry	*(Concerned now)* Then who did, because I closed it . . .
Helen	You're sure you closed it?
Larry	I'm certain I closed it.
Colm	I didn't open it – it was open when I got there.
Helen	*(Realising)* Oh my God.
Colm	*(To Helen)* And you were behind me . . .

A sudden sound off, distant stage left.

Helen	What's that?
Larry	*(Goes to the door. Listens. Then . . .)* Wait a

	minute! Wait a minute – I have it.
Helen	What?
Larry	If you three are not messing about this . . .
Colm	Swear to God, Larry.
Larry	Then I think I know who it is.
Aisling	Annie Ross?
Helen	Oh God . . .
Colm	Turn on the machine . . .
Helen	*(Of stage-right door)* Close that door . . .
Larry	To hell with the door – I know exactly who has come into the house . . .
Helen	Oh, Larry . . .
Larry	It's shagging William!
Colm	William?
Larry	Of course it's William – he never wanted us in here in the first place. He wants the house to himself, he's the only one with a key to the door and to the gate, the only one who can turn off the alarms . . .
Colm	No, I don't think . . .
Larry	And if you're not the messer who pushed the kitchen door in on me . . .
Colm	Swear to God, Larry.
Larry	Then it has to be him. He's back in the house.

Another sound off. Larry goes again to the stage-left door and opens it.

| Helen | Larry, where are you going? |
| Larry | I'm going to get the bastard, to give him the surprise of his shaggin' life. |

225

Helen	Larry, it's very dark out there . . .
Colm	Larry, I wouldn't . . .
Larry	No one's asking you to. *(Going)* I had my suspicions of this all along . . .
Helen	But Larry, what about recording the midnight haunting?
Larry	This is better than any haunting – the phantom of the opera in the old house, exposed.
Colm	Here, take this torch . . .

A sound, off

| Larry | *(Whispers)* There he is again – the one-eyed bastard. No, keep the torch – I'll leave this door open. This'll frighten the shite out of him. |

Larry goes quietly through the stage-left door, leaving it open. Looks back in.

| Larry | *(Whispers)* May be best if you turn the recorder on anyway – get me dragging him in . . . *(Goes)* |

Pause

Helen	Colm?
Colm	Maybe he's right.
Aisling	Much colder now, isn't it?
Colm	Because the door is open.
Aisling	And does anyone get that smell?

The stage-left door suddenly slams shut. They look at each other.

Helen	*(Nervously)* Why did he do that – shut the door?
Colm	Maybe . . . maybe he wants to surprise him.
Helen	But it's pitch black out there.
Aisling	I think she's here.
Helen	*(Angrily)* Aisling, will you stop saying that – you know as well as any of us that there's nothing.

A flash of lightning and an immediate crack of thunder. The lights flicker and go dim.

Helen	Oh my God – do you have the torch, Colm?
Colm	Yes, yes – the recorder, turn the recorder on.
Helen	Oh, right. *(She nervously presses the button)* There.

A crack of thunder and, as it fades, there is now, in the room, the sound of a girl gently sobbing.

Colm	Oh, Jesus Christ.
Aisling	Hello? Where are you? *(Looks around)*
Helen	Oh, Jesus help us – this is awful.
Colm	Just don't move, anyone – stay exactly where you are.
Aisling	Annie . . . Annie Ross?
Colm	*(Suddenly angry)* Oh for Christ's sake – Helen!
Helen	*(Jumps)* What is it?
Colm	That sobbing is coming from the tape-recorder – look, you pressed PLAY instead of RECORD. That's the old sobbing on the tape. *(Angrily turns it off)*
Helen	Oh. Sorry.
Colm	Jesus Christ Almighty. *(Presses RECORD)* Will you try to be more careful.

Helen	I said sorry!
Aisling	There's that smell again – does anyone else get that smell?
Colm	No, we don't!
Helen	*(Then)* No, Colm, there *is* a smell – there's definitely a smell . . . a sweet smell . . .
Colm	What?
Helen	No, there is – there really is . . .
Colm	*(Sniffs)* Oh Christ, you're right – there is . . .
Helen	*(Hands to her face)* Oh wait! I know what it is. *(Smells her hands)* It's the cream – it's the cream I put on Larry's scalded hand.
Colm	For God's sake, Helen, what are you at? What are you trying to do!
Helen	I'm sorry – I never had a chance to wash it off . . .
Aisling	I don't think it's that.
Colm	*(Nervously)* Is it me, or are those lights dimming?
Helen	Yes . . . yes they are . . .
Colm	Probably that electrical storm coming in.
Aisling	*(Looking around)* There really is something going to happen.
Helen	Will you stop saying that!

The lights have now dimmed very low. Now the sound of heavy breathing is heard.

Colm	What's that? It's someone breathing – it's someone breathing heavily . . . Listen.
Helen	*(Comes from the shadows)* It's me, Colm, I'm here!
Colm	Christ, Helen, how can you be so stupid!

Helen	Oh, I'm sorry – but I have to breathe!
Colm	All right! *(Then)* OK, don't worry, if the lights go, I have the torch and . . .
Aisling	*(Quietly)* Annie? Are you here? Annie Ross?

Suddenly, away in the house, there is a very frightened roar. Immediately, footsteps are heard outside the stage-left door. Now the stage-right door slams shut and the handle of the stage-left door begins to turn furiously, as though against a locked door. The lights go out. Now the stage-left door is being kicked and pounded and hit with some force. A crack of thunder and lightning – and Colm swings the beam of the torch around in the darkness. All as:

Colm	*(Shouts)* Who's there? Who's there? Larry, is that you?
Helen	*(Shouts)* Turn the torch on! Larry? Where's Larry? Larry?
Aisling	*(Calls out)* Annie Ross! Thank you, Annie Ross, thank you for coming.
Helen	*(To Aisling)* Will you shut up! *(To Colm)* Colm, she's trying to get in.
Colm	*(Roars)* Where's my knife?
Helen	*(Shouts)* Go away, leave us alone, go away!
Aisling	*(Joyfully)* Yes! Yes! Yes! Thank you for coming.
Helen	*(Hysterical)* Turn on the lights!

The lights suddenly come on and the stage-left door bursts open. Larry runs in and stands, dishevelled, out of breath. Colm is hiding under a table, Helen also hiding, Aisling is standing with her arms outstretched.

Larry	*(Looks. Quietly)* Bastards! You shower of bastards!
Helen	*(Emerging)* Larry, what's happening? What happened out there?
Larry	Like you don't know?
Colm	*(Emerging)* Was it William?
Larry	*(Hard)* No, Colm, it wasn't William. The door down there is locked, the alarms are still on, no one has come into this house tonight . . . except a gang of shagging comedians!
Helen	But Larry . . .
Larry	Who think it's great fun to slam that door and lock me out there and hold it shut and me out there in the pitch black . . .
Helen	No, Larry . . .
Larry	Yes, Helen – you and your latest hero.
Colm	But none of us . . .
Larry	None of you what? None of you went after me, turning off lights, running past me in the dark . . .
Aisling	*(Hopefully)* Oh God.
Larry	. . . touching me, whispering into my face, pulling at my shirt, having the time of your lives . . .
Helen	Larry, we were all in here . . .
Larry	. . . and then running back in here by the backstairs to leave me roaring out there . . .
Helen	What backstairs?
Larry	Or was it just him *(Colm)*, was it? The funny man, the great explorer?
Colm	No!
Helen	No, Larry, none of us . . .

Larry	And you are some liar, Helen – as if I didn't know that already . . .
Colm	Now Larry, you listen here . . .
Larry	*(To Colm)* And I'm sick and tired of you, smart-arse, because you have been goading me all night with your debates and your poetry and your bungee jump and am I a man or a woman . . .
Helen	Larry, he wasn't . . .
Larry	And I'm sick of you too, Helen – running around with the latest Bobby Andrews in front of my bloody face . . .
Colm	*(Angrily)* Now Larry, you listen to me . . . *(Holds the knife towards Larry)*
Larry	No, I will not listen to you – *(Cracks)* and don't you point that shagging knife at me! Bastard!
Helen	Larry! Don't!

Larry runs at Colm. The struggle is brief, Colm is taken off guard. The knife falls. All as:

Larry	Bastard! *(Hits Colm and grabs the knife)* Smart-arse bastard . . .
Helen	No, Larry! No!

Larry has grabbed Colm from behind by the hair and now, with Colm on his knees, Larry holds the knife to his throat. Everything stops. All suddenly quiet.

Larry	No jokes now, eh? Now we're all very serious, aren't we?

231

Helen	Larry, please darling, you've had much too much to drink . . . and none of us were out there . . .
Larry	Oh, I imagined it all, did I?
Helen	Darling, you really could have – that medication is very strong . . .
Larry	Yes, and why am I on that medication, Helen?
Helen	I know, Larry.
Larry	*(To Colm)* Do you know, Mr Funny man?
Colm	*(Paralysed with fear)* Larry, that blade is very sharp . . .
Larry	Is it? And is it as sharp as the syringe that I had held against my throat for five shagging minutes, is it?
Colm	I'm sure it is, Larry.
Larry	And do you know what that did to me . . . ?
Colm	Yes, Larry . . .
Larry	That I went from being an up-and-coming executive to being the gobshite of the office, passed over for every appointment . . .
Helen	No, Larry . . .
Larry	. . . put on medication that turned me into a zombie by day and a sexual joke in bed at night . . .
Helen	No, Larry . . .
Larry	Yes, Helen! Why else are Bobby Andrews and all the others still around?
Helen	Larry, that is not true . . .
Colm	Please, Larry . . .
Larry	*(To Colm)* And then there's you, trying to frighten the shite out of me all over again . . .
Colm	But I didn't – and, Larry, there's something I

232

	really want to tell you, something that will really help you.
Larry	*(Stops)* Oh, and what's that?
Colm	Just, please, don't move the knife . . .
Larry	All right, speak up so, I'm all ears. *(Moves the knife to Colm's ear)* Though you won't be if this is another one of your jokes.
Colm	It's not, it's not . . .
Helen	Larry, don't!
Aisling	*(Panic)* Oh Jesus, I hate seeing people having their ears cut off.
Larry	Oh, used to that in your business, are you, Aisling?
Aisling	No, only once in a film when this fellow had a butcher's knife and . . .
Colm	For Christ's sake, shut up.
Helen	Shut up, Aisling.
Larry	So go on, Colm – but you give me a joke and I'll give you your ear.
Colm	It's not a joke, Larry, it's the truth. *(Then)* I know you're worried that the fellow who had the hypodermic was never caught and that he threatened to come and get you . . .
Larry	Oh, thanks for reminding me.
Colm	But that's the thing, he won't – because months ago, at the school, we heard who he was – a real tearaway, into drugs and everything – and we heard he had gone off to Holland and that, last April, he died of Aids, so he's gone and he'll never be back to do anything to you.
Larry	And you never told anyone this?
Colm	We heard it in confidence from his mother.

Larry	And I'm supposed to believe this, am I?
Aisling	Oh, please don't cut off his ear.
Colm	Will you shut up!
Helen	Shut up, Aisling!
Colm	I wanted to tell you earlier, but you wouldn't listen to me.
Helen	Oh Larry, if he's dead, then . . .
Colm	And it's God's truth, Larry.
Helen	Darling, you must believe Colm if he's saying it.
Larry	*(To Helen)* Oh, must I? The same, I suppose, as I must believe everything you tell me?
Helen	What?
Larry	Like when you tell me you're off every Thursday night making lampshades, I'm to believe that too, am I?
Helen	But I do make lampshades every Thursday.
Larry	*(Angrily)* And I shagging know you don't!
Colm	My ear . . . !
Helen	But Larry, I do!
Larry	You were shagging seen, Helen . . .
Helen	Seen? Seen where?
Larry	Along Brighton Avenue, where Bobby Andrews happens to live.
Helen	*(Amazed)* On a Thursday?
Larry	Yes, on a Thursday, and you better admit it because I'm fed up being made a fool of.
Colm	Helen, for Christ's sake, admit it.
Helen	But it's not true . . .
Larry	*(Switches the knife back to Colm's throat)* I'm not a fool, Helen!
Aisling	Oh Jesus, I hate seeing blood squirting out . . .

Colm	*(Shouts to Aisling)* Will you shut up! *(To Helen)* And will you admit it!
Helen	But I do make lampshades on a Thursday.
Larry	You don't!
Aisling	She does, she does, she does, she does! It's on a Monday she doesn't make anything.
Helen	Will you shut up!
Aisling	It's on a Monday she doesn't make pottery.
Helen	I do!
Aisling	*(To Helen)* You don't – you go to see your aunt Brigid dying.
Helen	I don't.
Aisling	Your aunt Maggie then.
Helen	I don't – I make pottery . . .
Aisling	She doesn't . . .
Larry	She does!
Aisling	No, she buys them . . .
Larry	She doesn't! And I don't give a shite about Monday, I want to know about Thursday *(Pulls Colm's head back)* and I want it *now* or this bastard is dead!
Colm	*(Panic)* Helen!
Helen	*(Shouts)* All right, all right, all right! If that's what you want. I don't go to a class on a Thursday; I don't go. All right? Now are you satisfied? I don't go! OK?
Colm	*(After a pause. Quietly)* Larry, you're moving the knife without meaning to.
Larry	You see, Helen, I knew you didn't go.
Aisling	No, she . . .
Helen	Shut up.

Aisling	And I'm fed up with being told to shut up.
Colm	Shut up, Aisling. Go on, Helen!
Helen	But Larry, as God is my judge, I don't see Bobby Andrews on a Thursday . . .
Larry	*(Angrily)* Now, Helen . . .
Helen	I don't! I'll tell you what I do: I visit Kathy Fleming. Every Thursday I visit her, Kathy Fleming . . . and I buy those lampshades, all of them, and I pretend I made them, pretend I painted them and everything. All right?
Larry	But why would you visit Kathy Fleming?
Helen	Because . . . because she's an old friend and because Victor Fleming is your boss and could be interviewing you, and she could be an influence . . .
Larry	And why did you never tell me this?
Helen	For the same reason, Larry, as I do everything – because I don't want to humiliate you, because I want you back on your feet, with your pride, to give you that, at least.
Larry	*(Relaxes the knife)* And Bobby Andrews?
Helen	Tennis, Larry. Saturday mornings, mixed doubles, nothing more, ever. Jesus.
Larry	*(Pause)* And this really is the truth, Helen?
Helen	*(Gently)* What more can I say? Ring up Kathy – ask her.

Larry has lowered the knife. Colm sees his opportunity and suddenly grabs and twists Larry's burned hand and wrist. Larry is caught off guard. The knife falls.

236

Colm	Now, you bastard . . .
Helen	Colm, let him go . . .
Aisling	Leave him alone! *(Picks up the knife)*
Colm	I'm only after getting over dying, and you do this to me! *(Throws Larry down)*
Helen	Leave him alone!
Colm	*(Pushes Helen away)* Get away from me. *(Kicks Larry)* Bastard.
Aisling	*(Holding the knife)* Leave him alone.
Helen	He can't fight back.
Colm	*(Kicks Larry again)* Bastard . . . bastard . . .
Aisling	*(Screams, holding the knife high)* I said, leave him alone! Leave him alone! Leave him alone!

Aisling runs at Colm, the knife held high. Colm grabs her wrist. Larry lies helpless. Helen stands. Immediately a flash of lightning strobes across the room and there is a crack of thunder. The room suddenly seems possessed and Larry, Helen, Colm and Aisling watch in horror as the wheelchair is lifted from the ground, the two doors bang open and closed, the large tree crashes against the window outside, the light above swings back and forth. Aisling's scream has now been taken up and seems to reverberate endlessly throughout the house into a long, loud scream from elsewhere – as though a greater, more angry force is now present in the room. It all stops as suddenly as it started.

Helen   My God.

Immediate blackout

End of Act Two, Scene One

237

Act Two

Scene Two

In the darkness, we hear some of the 'interview' dialogue from the beginning of this scene. When the lights come up, it is the next morning, 9.30 am. The sleeping bags have been used. There is the remains of some food and general disorder. The sun shines in. We now see clearly where the great tree has fallen across the window, but not broken it.

Aisling sits applying her make-up. Helen is tidying, filling a bin liner and polishing. Colm is putting books away, also packing his overnight bag. He has a large plaster and lint on his face. He now seems nervous and quick-tempered.

The mood is subdued. All are listening (as are we) to the radio: Gerry Ryan interviewing Larry.

Gerry	But you're not actually in the house now, Larry, are you?
Larry	No, Gerry, I'm outside in the front garden – the thing is, for some mysterious reason, my mobile won't work inside the house at all.
Gerry	Oh, I see. So how did you actually get out if you're all locked in?
Larry	The caretaker, William, just arrived and he

turned off the alarms and opened the door . . .

Gerry   Great – and now, Larry, I'm told the courier has just arrived in the studio with your tape.

Larry   Oh good.

Gerry   This is the tape, folks, that we asked Larry to make, telling us exactly how it felt to be in that room at the exact time of the haunting. So, Larry, while we're getting that lined up – and, folks, believe me, this will be one spooky tape – tell us, Larry, what is it like just standing there, looking at the house where Annie Ross went fairly bonkers last night – like, does it look any different?

Larry   Well, the big tree was thrown against the house . . .

Gerry   But that wouldn't have been the storm, would it?

Larry   It's possible – but inside the house, she really broke up the place – wrecked the plumbing, flooded the basement . . .

Gerry   God Almighty, didn't like you being in there did she?

Larry   No, she did not, Gerry.

Gerry   And the four of you were fairly thrown around during all this?

Larry   Oh, like rag dolls. One of us, fellow called Colm, has a big gash on his head.

Gerry   My God – but fair dues to you, you all lasted out the night . . .

Larry   Well, it's all for a good cause, Gerry, all for the Starving Children of Africa and Asia.

Gerry   Indeed it is and I hear the pledges of money have been pouring in, so well done – but now, folks, pay attention to this – this is exactly how it sounded to be in that room, in that house, during the actual haunting. Listen to this, at twenty past eleven first, when the ghost of Annie Ross first came and then at midnight when she returned to try and finish them off. Listen up, folks.

We now hear, under, a recording of the dialogue from eleven-twenty, as:

Colm   *(Angrily)* And he talks about other people telling lies.

Helen   Larry knows what he has to do.

Colm   Yes, when he's not trying to slit open people's throats. And that tape has been hacked to pieces.

Helen   I think Larry did a great job editing it.

Colm   Yes – all night with his winding and unwinding and nobody getting a wink of sleep. Bastard.

Aisling   I didn't sleep either, especially after Annie Ross was here.

Colm   Listen, Aisling, you're not on the radio and neither am I – in here, we're allowed to tell the truth.

Aisling   But it is the truth, she was here.

Helen   Aisling, will you please shut up – I'm trying to hear this.

Aisling   I'm only saying I saw her.

Colm   And nobody else saw her?

Aisling   Well, that doesn't mean . . .

Colm   Face up to it – there was a storm, there were windows broken, there was a gale blowing

240

	through the place, it was all forecast, the house was hit by lightning, that tree is still scorched . . .
Aisling	But out there, Larry heard her running and whispering and . . .
Colm	Yes, when he was drunk, out of his head on medication, having another nervous breakdown . . .
Helen	Excuse me, Larry never had a breakdown and would you all shut up and listen to him.
Colm	You listen to him if you want to.
Helen	*(Takes the radio)* I will. And if you must know, I think he's great. And I'm proud of him, very proud of him.
Colm	*(Cutting)* Still think he'll get that job, do you?
Helen	*(Angrily)* I don't think it, Colm, I know it – you wait and see.

Helen goes out the stage-right door, with the radio.

Aisling	Is your face all right?
Colm	Stinging like hell, whatever cream she put on it. And look at my hands, they've never stopped shaking.
Aisling	I'm really sorry.
Colm	Forget it.
Aisling	I don't know what got into me.
Colm	*(Goes to the window)* Jesus, just look at him, the great executive – and they're going to give him the job? On his mobile, standing up to his knees in nettles.
Aisling	That's the only place where his phone would work.

241

Colm   *(Sarcastic)* Oh right – and I suppose that's Annie Ross again, making him suffer more, making him stand in nettles?

Aisling   Well, as a matter of fact . . .

William comes in, dressed as he was yesterday. He carries dust covers which, to the end, he will replace on the furniture.

Colm   Ah, William, you'll be delighted to hear that all your wishes came true – we had a miserable time.

William   Your friend is going to have to take responsibility for all the damage to this house . . .

Colm   He's no friend of mine.

William   *(Continuing)* . . . damage to the hall, damage to the doors, the back room upstairs has been pulled apart, the books have been ruined by water in the library, there are scorch marks on the floor outside . . .

Aisling   Where?

William   . . . and this will not be tolerated – the Hamilton family will want full compensation for all of this – and none of you will ever get permission to come in here again.

Colm   We'll be broken-hearted. *(With the wheelchair and books)* I'll leave these back.

William   Excuse me, sir, no going back to the library.

Colm   I'll only be two minutes.

William   Excuse me, your time is up in this house and, consequently, I now order you to leave.

Colm   *(Angrily)* And once I put these back, I'll be delighted to leave this kip forever. *(Goes)*

242

William	*(Calls)* You're acting in direct contravention of your agreement and that is duly noted.

William places some dust covers. Then:

Aisling	Excuse me. I saw her. *(No reply)* She was here last night and I saw her.
William	If that's your sleeping bag, kindly roll it up.
Aisling	*(Rolling up her sleeping bag)* And I think Jason Sweeney saw her as well. Did you ever see her, honestly?
William	*(Stops)* Look, miss, you may as well know, there is nothing here to see.
Aisling	No, there is.
William	There isn't and there never was and the sooner everybody realises that, the better – because I have a job to do here and this doesn't make it any easier.

Helen comes in with the radio, now turned off. She is excited and very confident.

Helen	Oh, hello, William – a wonderful night.
William	Your husband is going to have to take full responsibility for all of this.
Helen	Of course! *(Then)* Aisling, Larry was wonderful, full of confidence, just like his old self – and then they got Victor Fleming on.
Aisling	Who?
Helen	Victor Fleming. They got him on the phone on the programme – Larry's boss, Kathy's husband.

Aisling	Oh, the woman you visit on a Thursday.
Helen	Oh yes, and I must ring her and get that sorted out. But Victor came on and said they were all so proud of Larry and all the money he'd raised for Africa – and they've invited him over for lunchtime drinks at head office today.
Aisling	Well, that sounds good . . .
Helen	Absolutely – except that I think he should wait a few days before showing himself.
William	I expect you left the kitchen in as bad a state. Bloody savages.

William goes through stage-right door, to the kitchen. Helen busily clears up, as:

Aisling	And when you say you have to ring Kathy . . .
Helen	God, thanks for reminding me again, Aisling – I was so afraid that Larry would say on the radio that she and I were still great friends.
Aisling	Why, are you not?
Helen	Kathy? Haven't seen her for months.
Aisling	But you said that every Thursday . . .
Helen	Every Thursday, Aisling, I make lampshades.
Aisling	But you said to Larry, you . . .
Helen	On Thursdays, Aisling, I really do make lampshades, beautiful, hand-painted lampshades, and on Wednesday there really is literature appreciation, and on Tuesday rug-making . . .
Aisling	And on Monday?
Helen	And on Monday, let's just say . . .
Aisling	Bobby Andrews?

Helen	. . . that it would be better if you didn't ask. And anyway, that will all end if we get Bromley. My only real worry now is for today – that Victor Fleming won't be put off by Larry's appearance.
Aisling	Oh, his injuries?

Larry comes in stage-left door. He shows the signs of the fight: bruising on his face, his hand still bandaged, his clothes dishevelled. But, despite all, he is in great form.

Larry	Did you get it all on tape, Helen – Victor and everything?
Helen	Everything – and I was very proud of you, darling – you made a big impression.
Larry	And I intend to make an even bigger impression today.
Helen	Except that you do look a little battle-scarred for head office.
Larry	No, this'll tell them what I went through – they'll have to reward me for this.
Helen	Are you sure, darling?
Larry	Absolutely. And before you ask, I've taken my tablets this morning. *(Scratching his leg)* It's just these bloody nettle stings . . .
Helen	Oh, I think I have a cream for stings here.

She will get the cream and give it to Larry as:

Larry	*(Merrily)* I knew you would. *(To Aisling)* A big success, Aisling.

245

Aisling	Yes.
Larry	And strictly between us, I know you really think you saw something last night . . .
Aisling	Oh, but I did.
Larry	No, that's great, that's terrific, and great if you keep saying that, down at your hairdressers, at discos, at the chipper, wherever. And I want you to know that I think you were wonderful through all of this. Seriously.

Colm comes in to collect his bags.

Larry	Ah, Colm – did you hear the broadcast?
Colm	*(Coldly)* I heard enough of it.
Larry	It went first-class, better than we could have expected.
Colm	Really? Well I'm off, so goodbye and all that.
Larry	Oh right. *(Merrily)* And perfect weather for your bungee jump.
Colm	*(Angrily)* How the hell can I do a bungee jump shaking like this? Look at me – look at my hands. Haven't stop trembling . . .
Helen	Oh, I wouldn't have noticed.
Colm	And my head has been spinning – all thanks to you and your knife. The way I feel now, I've a good mind to crawl back to the school and ask for my job back.
Larry	Nonsense, Colm – you'll soon pull yourself together. Then you can go off and travel the world, enjoy your freedom, ask the dangerous questions, discover your sexuality, see what life

	can offer you, as Jean-Paul Sartre might say.
Colm	*(Coldly)* Right! *(Goes. Then stops)* Oh, and by the way, about that fellow with the hypodermic needle?
Larry	What?
Colm	Just that if I happen to see him around, I'll tell him you were asking for him.
Larry	What?
Colm	I'm sure he'll be delighted to meet you again, maybe visit you over in Bromley, maybe bring over a few of his pals with their syringes and finish you off. There's something to look forward to. Bye. *(Goes)*
Larry	But you said . . . *(Then laughs. Calls)* Ah, I get it – very good, Colm, very good. Still the comedian, eh? Still Mr Funny man? *(Concerned, to Helen)* That was a joke, wasn't it?
Helen	Of course it was – and now I think we should *allez*. *(Prepares to go)* Aisling, perhaps you'd say goodbye to William for us . . .
Aisling	Oh, right.
Helen	. . . and I must remember to drop him a little thank-you note. And thank you too for every-thing – a great night. *(She looks, to see Larry standing silently, concerned, looking after Colm)* Larry?
Larry	*(Roused)* Oh right, love. We're off, are we? Good. *(Anxiously, as he collects some belongings)* And, Helen, if we hurry, we might be able to catch up with Colm.
Helen	With Colm? For what?
Larry	*(Anxiously)* I just need to have a quiet word with him about what he was saying there . . .

Helen	*(Annoyed)* Oh, for God's sake, Larry – he was only joking.
Larry	*(Very anxious)* Yes, yes, I know, but I just need to be sure, just need to be certain about all that before I do anything . . . before I see Fleming, before I commit myself to anything. If . . . if we hurry we'll catch him. I'll . . . I'll ask him nicely and . . . and please, I'd really like you to be there to hear what he says, please. *(Goes, calling)* Colm?
Helen	*(Sudden outburst of pent-up anger)* Oh for Christ's sake, Larry, not this all over again! How can we expect to get anywhere if you keep going back to the same bloody carry-on? Because I can't take much more and I'm not going to! *(Stops, aware of Aisling. Very sweetly)* Ah, Aisling, yes, and hopefully see you soon. *(Going)*
Aisling	Yeah. And next Monday, you'll be in for your appointment as usual?
Helen	*(Stops. Sadly)* We'll see, Aisling, we'll see.
Larry	*(Far off and angrily)* Helen!
Helen	*(Resigned)* Coming, Larry, coming. *(Goes)*

Aisling waits for William. He comes in.

William	Locking up now. *(Continues with the dust covers)*
Aisling	Right. *(Then)* The others are gone.
William	*(Grumpily)* Good!
Aisling	*(Her opportunity)* Can I ask you something? Do you really not believe that the spirit of Annie Ross . . . ?

William	Sorry, miss – it's past your time here and . . .
Aisling	I'm only asking because Mrs Campion . . .
William	*(Harder)* Miss, I need to be locking up now . . .
Aisling	No, it's just what she told me about Annie . . .
William	And I have my instructions . . .
Aisling	About how Stephen Hamilton wanted to marry her until she got pregnant . . .
William	Miss, you have to go now.
Aisling	. . . but then he said he'd marry her if she had an abortion . . .
William	*(Finally)* Miss, I don't have time for . . .
Aisling	*(Louder)* And I always knew just how Annie felt, because the very same thing happened to me.
William	*(Stops)* What did you say?
Aisling	No one knows; I always say I lost my baby, but I didn't . . . it was all because my mammy was dead and my boyfriend didn't want me. So I know how Annie Ross felt when she lost everything, when she went and had . . . you know. So I know.
William	*(Quietly)* You know nothing.
Aisling	No, I do, but I won't tell anyone, I won't blurt it out – but last night I'm sure I saw her – and that means I saw my mammy too . . . *(Stops)* But I wanted to ask you, do you really think these spirits – that the spirit of Annie is around, in here?
William	*(Pause. Then, quietly)* Course it is.
Aisling	Really? Honestly?
William	Always been here.
Aisling	I knew it! And she was just like me . . .

249

William	She was nothing like you.
Aisling	No, I mean in the way we both like to look nice and people think we're not too bright and our fellows didn't want us and when we both found we were going to have our babies, we both had to . . .
William	That's what I mean. She didn't.
Aisling	Pardon?
William	She had her child. Annie did.
Aisling	No – Mrs Campion said she had . . . *('an abortion' is implied)*
William	*(Continues with the dust covers)* They thought she had, but she didn't.
Aisling	What?
William	She had the baby, premature, gave it to her sister and came back, said nothing, and they were none the wiser. And the baby grew up, in London, place called Willesden. *(Pause)* A little fellow, he was.
Aisling	*(Then, realising)* You. You're her child.
William	Little fellow with a funny eye and a funny leg. Bad time for her to be running off to London – too late for one thing, too early for the other.
Aisling	Oh God.
William	But they're a good family, the Hamiltons – they came looking for me, wasn't easy, but they found me and gave me this job.
Aisling	Then you're really . . . ? You have the right to all . . . *('this house and property' is implied)*
William	*(Harder)* And quite happy doing what I'm doing, never wanted for anything else. *(Then)* And now, miss, I'll be locking up.

Suddenly some books fall over from the bookshelf, onto the floor. Aisling looks, then looks to William.

William Don't mind that. It happens. Nothing to worry about.

Aisling No. *(Suddenly goes to him and kisses him)* Thank you for telling me all that. *(Determined)* And I won't tell a soul.

William Don't.

Aisling I won't, honestly, I won't! Bye. *(Going)*

William Goodbye. And listen – you keep your spirits up. All right?

Aisling Yes. And you too.

Aisling goes. William looks around the room. All the dust covers are now in place again. Suddenly, behind him, the stage-right door slams over and then opens again. William turns and looks at it. He smiles.

William Stop worrying – she won't tell anybody. Go to sleep – you've had a busy night.

The door now begins to close over very gently. When it is shut, William nods, satisfied. He goes through the stage-left door, closing it behind him, as the girl's voice sings the ending of the song: 'I don't want to play in your yard/if you won't be good to me' as we fade to darkness.

The End